KEEPING THE CUSTOMER SATISFIED —
A GUIDE TO FIELD SERVICE

KEEPING THE CUSTOMER SATISFIED —
A GUIDE TO FIELD SERVICE

Eastman Kodak Company

ASQC Quality Press
American Society for Quality Control
310 West Wisconsin Avenue
Milwaukee, Wisconsin 53203

Kew Garden Hills

KEEPING THE CUSTOMER SATISFIED — A GUIDE TO FIELD SERVICE

Eastman Kodak Company

Contributing Authors
William J. Trimble and Robert W. Duncan
Customer Equipment Services, Eastman Kodak Company

Published by ASQC Quality Press • Milwaukee

Acquisitions Editor: Jeanine L. Lau
Production Editor: Tammy Griffin
Cover design: Ponsbach Design. Set in Baskerville by The Typesetter.
Printed and bound by BookCrafters.

10987654321
ISBN 0-87389-053-1

Printed in the United States of America

12/26/00

Contents

Preface

Is equipment service a commodity? People go into an appliance store to buy a television set where they can observe the characteristics of each one. Based on these observations, they can make a decision about which set to buy. In this respect, a television set is a technological commodity. The consumer is able to turn the television set on, look at its picture, listen to its sound, and tune in different channels. In short, consumers know before the purchase exactly what they are getting for their money. The consumer is able to measure the value at the time of purchase.

When a service contract is purchased, the value cannot be measured until the service is performed. The service being purchased cannot be *tried out* to assess its value ahead of time. It can only be compared to similar former circumstances of service need. Servicing high-technology products complicates the situation even more. The lack of visible indicators for the operation of the equipment makes servicing these products seem like magic. Service contracts for high-technology products take the form of insurance policies that a customer buys. Just as with insurance companies, service is purchased based on the reputation of the service organization.

The real focus of service is to satisfy customer needs by servicing the equipment that is giving customers a competitive edge in their industry. By keeping the customer's "technological commodities" running at peak performance, the field engineer and the service organization as a whole are adding value to the product. While this book stresses technology in servicing products in a field service environment, it is important to remember that the ultimate goal of any service organization is to maintain or enhance the customer's satisfaction with the products. Technology is only a tool that is used to maintain the customer's perception of high-quality products.

The goal of *Keeping the Customer Satisfied — A Guide to Field Service* is to provide insight into current service technologies that have application in reaching a solution to the service dilemma created by our technological environment. It is not intended to provide an in-depth study of every topic, or to be a self-teach course or a "how to" book for solving field service problems brought on by new technology. This book is intended to be a thought-provoker that gives some insights into how to deal effectively with new technology products and notes areas of concern to field service managers both today and in the near future.

The material presented here represents the opinions of the writers, based on years of experience in a field service organization. William J. Trimble has an extensive background in computer applications and computer technology. He has been involved with computer design and the service of computers for more than 25 years with Eastman Kodak Company, some of which were spent in the Kodak Research Labs. Robert W. Duncan has extensive background servicing computers and computer-controlled devices. Following his graduation from Lehigh University with a bachelor of science degree in electrical engineering, he joined the Customer Equipment Services Division of Eastman Kodak Company. Trimble and Duncan wish to thank the many people in Eastman Kodak Company, especially those in the Customer Equipment Services organization, who have helped in producing this book.

Introduction

Service must now support technological commodities, while remaining focused on the customer.

We are living during a computer and electronic revolution. Almost every aspect of daily life is being influenced by the applications of computers in our environment. Even those who do not use a computer during their average day cannot escape the impact of the computer, and the software that drives it, on many aspects of their daily lives. Computers and computer-driven devices appear to be everywhere. From a simple digital wristwatch to the controls of appliances, automobiles, and nearly every electronic device we encounter, the computer is taking control.

The world has gone digital under the control and logical decision-making process of the computer. As time itself is marked, it is now counted in precise digital terms. How long has it been since the digital wristwatch changed the way we tell time? What several years ago was described as twenty-five minutes to four o'clock is now precisely described as three thirty-five. The microelectronic chips have added precision to our ways of describing the simplest events.

While some may consider an environment supported by computers to be an easier, more productive, and maybe even more desirable environment, the increasing dependence on the computer has greatly influenced life itself. Sometimes our dependence on computers leaves us practically helpless to complete necessary tasks when the computer system fails. We tend now to view such failures as crises that need immediate attention by qualified service technicians.

Many appliances and products were for years a "tinkerer's dream." When failures occurred, a turn of a screw here, or a tap with a hammer there, could often repair a pesky appliance. The computer and micro-electronics have changed that and outdated the home repair of many appliances which are seemingly critical to daily life. Probably one of the most visible examples exists in the television industry.

In the early days of television, when the set failed, it was possible for the owner to carefully mark each tube and then take the tubes to the local drugstore to test. If a weak tube was found, the home television "expert" would simply replace the suspect tube and usually would be watching a television program in a matter of hours.

The technology of today's television receiver prohibits this approach entirely. Completely solid state television sets make the service task a job for only the trained technician with sophisticated test equipment. Not only are the replaceable parts more expensive, but the density of these components is far greater in the current state-of-the-art television receiver.

Service personnel providing service support for almost any new product must cope with the applications of computer technology and the service crises this technology creates. The dilemma is how to provide — efficiently and economically — the customer with the quality of service that will satisfy his or her needs while dealing with the complexities of these new technologies in an economically attractive way.

Because of the wide presence of computers, the service industry is also facing an increasingly sophisticated base of customers. This sophistication is due to the daily communication customers have with the logical, precise format of the computer. In addition, customers are coming to expect more from products because *computers can do anything.* The decision process of logical reasoning experienced by the customer when dealing with a computer interface becomes an approach to solving humanistic problems and creates customer demands which strive for perfection. Customers no longer accept the error rates, quality, and reliability that were associated with the tinkerer's world of yesterday. They expect digital perfection, and they are getting it!

The intent of *Keeping the Customer Satisfied — A Guide to Field Service* is to provide insight into current service technologies that have application in reaching a solution to the service dilemma created by our technological environment. Field service, as discussed throughout this book, is defined as the performance of preventive or corrective maintenance to ensure that a product operates in the environment it was designed for, to specification, for its intended lifetime.

There is no single solution to the service problems created by our technological environment that is applicable to all situations, but through a combination of service technologies and diagnostic approaches, the problems facing the field engineer may be minimized.

1

History—The Changing Field Service Environment

The customer always has been, and always will be, the measure of service effectiveness.

History

Product and support service to customers dates back to times when a local town craftsman provided repair for the goods he produced. The repeat business enjoyed by these independent manufacturers, with their various products, was not unlike the repeat business experienced today by major industry, where dependable and affordable service is a major influence in the consumer's purchasing decisions.

Reliability Is the Key

Customers have insisted on reliable products for a long time. The names of some manufacturers have become closely associated with particular types of products as a result of the quality of both the product and service these manufacturers provide.

When a customer purchased goods from a local craftsman, a one-to-one relationship was established with not only the manufacturer of the product, but also with the expert in the product's construction and operation. Any problem with a customer's purchase was quickly resolved and customer satisfaction was easily established. As business expanded, the servicing of products became a larger and larger portion of the daily work of these independent manufacturers. Therefore, to continue manufacturing it was important to provide good product reliability, while servicing the products that failed.

Change and Revolution

The extensive mass production that came about during World War II appears to have been the catalyst that started the service industry as we know it today. The quality built into the products was no longer the result of one individual's efforts, but the result of the contributions of a group of craftspeople and assembly-line personnel. The products were widely distributed and, therefore, the actual builder of the product was not available when repairs were required. This led to the need for repair people or field engineers throughout the country. These field engineers could provide the product support and repair service at the customer's location.

The Field Engineer

A field engineer in "precomputer times" required only product operation knowledge and primarily mechanical know-how. The operation of most products was relatively straightforward, requiring little training or specialized background. The operational cycle of a product could be easily observed and problems located when the cycle was interrupted.

This type and level of service support has been all that was necessary for decades. The most complex devices generally were supported by factory-trained engineers, but larger volume consumer items required only a good mechanic.

How things have changed in the last 10 to 15 years! Service now requires much more than just a good mechanic. Product knowledge must now be supplemented by sophisticated diagnostic procedures, expensive test equipment, and service approaches that allow for the evaluation of the product's operation.

Changes in Product Complexity

In order to provide competitive features in a cost-effective manner, the mechanical control sections of many products have been replaced by electronics of one form or another. It is this transition that has created the service support problems that face manufacturers today. The complexity of products is currently being increased by the application of computers to perform many formerly mechanical functions. This is made possible (and economical) by the decreasing cost of these components and the dramatic improvements in their performance. This performance improvement can be better understood through a review of the evolution of computers in the 1970s.

Evolution of the Computer

Changes in the power of the computer over the last decade have required similar changes in service approaches and service technology. As computers mature, the challenges to the service industry are becoming greater. From minicomputers to microcomputers and now mini- and micro-mainframes, the basic operations of a computer have remained the same. By processing only ones and zeros (or highs and lows, if you wish), the computer performs thousands, and even millions of operations in a second. Several analogies to the speed of manual calculations have been made. To illustrate this computer processing speed versus manual speed, several interesting analogies have been made:

- In the first generation of computers, events were measured in milliseconds. If a person could perform one addition each second, it would require 17 minutes to complete 1,000 additions. The first generation computers could complete the same number of additions in only one second.

- The second generation computers were much faster and could complete the same addition in about 1 microsecond. This allowed the computer to accomplish one million additions in 1 second. A person performing one addition per second would need almost 12 days to complete the one million additions.

- Computers commonly available today can complete the same addition in about 1 nanosecond. That speed results in approximately one billion additions per second. A person performing one addition per second would not complete these additions for nearly 32 years.

- Emerging technologies in the computer industry are allowing for further processing speed increases. The more sophisticated computers are approaching the capability of performing additions at a rate of one each picosecond. This equates to one thousand billion additions per second. If we compare this to a person making one addition per second, the span of time to finish one thousand billion additions would be 317 centuries.

From these analogies, we can easily realize the advancement of computer technology. As the performance of these processors has improved, a similar degree of progress has been made in the peripheral devices they control to accomplish tasks.

History of Microelectronics

The early computers of the 1960s were transistorized versions of much larger vacuum-tube devices. Computers of this decade were restricted by the then current state of the art to 8 bits of address and data logic. Although these machines were, and still are, used for machine control applications, they lacked versatility when compared to their much larger ancestors. Medium-scale integrated circuitry provided more capability by reducing the area required for logic functions. This made possible the 16-bit mini-computer, which had capabilities similar to those of the much larger computers. The 16-bit minicomputer is the most widely used computer for product control and numerical data reduction today.

Large Scale Integration (LSI) became state of the art in the late 1960s. Applying LSI technologies to the reduction of the area needed for logic functions resulted in the first 4-bit microcomputers. These first micro-computers were limited in their versatility because of their address and data storage capabilities. Further enhancements to LSI made the 8-bit micro-processor practical. These enhancements provided the microprocessor with increased flexibility and a larger number of possible applications. However, in order to provide the necessary computer functions, a large number of support chips was required.

Very Large Scale Integration (VLSI) became a reality during the early 1970s and made it possible to design support circuitry into the microprocessor. The first entry was a 4-bit microprocessor. These devices included techniques used in minicomputer design and integrated the support functions onto the same chip. The number of bits available, however, represented the most serious limitation. This limitation was soon overcome by 8-bit architectures. Now micro-processors with 8-bit architecture could be compared to the functional equivalent of the early 8-bit minicomputers.

Expanded Use and Applications

Important changes were also occurring at the same time in the applications of these microelectronic devices. As the sophistication of the microprocessor increased, the uses it found also increased. Early devices were limited in their application when compared to later LSI technology. The peripheral components required to operate these early devices and the cumbersome software development procedures greatly increased the product's overhead costs associated with these microprocessors. Therefore, limited demand made a long-term commitment to these devices unattractive to vendors and manufacturers. This lack of long-term production commitment and the limited application of these early microprocessors created parts-stocking problems and service problems due to their relatively short manufacturing life cycles.

Control Intelligence and Storage

Input and Output (I/O) control devices have become very intelligent. They can be programmed to perform specialized tasks and, in computer terms, unburden the Central Processing Unit (CPU). This results in an increase in the computer's processing capacity and a performance level not possible without intelligent I/O control. A peripheral device can be initialized by the central computer and then turned on or off quickly to either input or output data. In the case of a printer, a stream of data can be sent at one time to the printer and then, while the intelligence of the printer produces the final output, the central computer can continue processing information in a parallel time frame.

Another area of great change is in the storage capacities of computers. Addressing megabytes of storage locations directly is now common. This has allowed for the faster execution of software routines and the addition of many features to a product through the expanded memory available. As the speed of the computer increases, the amount of data it can process also increases, requiring more storage space. In many of today's applications, the storage space available still determines the features and functions that are possible.

Summary

The demands on field service have changed dramatically since the earliest products were supported by the craftsman who made the product. Dealing with the problems of complex computer-driven equipment was the catalyst for applying technology to the support of field service.

2

New Technology Causes New "Bugs"

Providing service for new technology-driven products can lead the service organization to concentrate more on the technology than on the customer.

Not many years ago, a circuit diagram for a product could be analyzed for serviceability or testability by an electrical engineer applying standard logic techniques of circuit analysis. For example, an AND gate was a structure of known and predictable operation. The engineer encountering this symbol on a circuit diagram knew exactly how it functioned in the circuit. Tests to evaluate the performance of this gate were relatively straightforward when compared to current solid state devices. In today's solid state devices there are new "bugs." These bugs may be in the form of hardware, software, or system problems. They require special attention by the engineer designing either testability approaches or diagnostic procedures for a product or a portion of a product. A circuit diagram can no longer identify the circuit's operation by itself.

Electrical Software

The purpose or function of many solid state devices is now determined by the software control of the devices. A pure evaluation of the components often does not even give a clue to their purpose or operation in a circuit without additional information about the control of the components. A single integrated circuit may be used to input data or to output data, or both. How the device performs functionally in a circuit is now dictated by the software control and status "words" sent to the device. This adds a new dimension to the term *circuit analysis*, to the practice of circuit analysis, and to the world of electrical and service engineering. Systems knowledge is now a requirement to meet the expectations in either engineering area fully.

The new bugs are everywhere, from the control of a peripheral device, to the primary interfaces, to a main product function. The advent of software set up to control device functionality is presenting new service and design challenges.

Challenge to Field Engineers

A field engineer is, at best, poorly prepared to deal with the problems created by these software/hardware interfaces. It is becoming extremely difficult to determine when software programmable integrated circuits are performing properly. The necessary data and tools are seldom available to the field engineer for a complete circuit operational analysis, as are the training and skills required to perform the analysis. The investment to make this knowledge available is often beyond what most service organizations are willing to commit to. Therefore, the operation of complex electronic components is becoming increasingly vague to field service personnel.

The result of the new bugs is a change in basic service and repair philosophy. The current trend is away from component level fault isolation and toward board level and subassembly diagnosis and repair or replacement. The hope here in simplifying field repair is to reduce the need for sophisticated test equipment and training for each service person. Diagnosing and repairing to the board or subassembly level today is not unlike replacing tubes in early electronic products.

An Alternative

There are alternatives available to assist in coping with these new bugs. One alternative which provides a means to isolate these equipment failures is to provide the service person with procedural diagnostics and testability criteria. This involves including the *service intelligence* either in the product or in an external delivery device (i.e., a portable computer). The need for such approaches to provide service support for complex products has been influenced by several factors both of an environmental and technological nature. In order to increase the understanding of this current dilemma and provide a possible approach to addressing this problem, a review of the causes and past experience may be helpful.

Microelectronics

We have stated that the service business and the environment in which it is carried out have been significantly affected by the drastic technological changes of the last decade and a half. Many indicators point to a continuing change in these technologies. The primary influence on this changing environment has been the advent of microelectronics.

Microelectronic advances, to a large degree, have been made possible through the use of the computer. A significant result of microelectronic applications in the minicomputer was the micro-computer, which has been incorporated into new products. These microcomputers contribute to the way new technology has influenced the business and environment of the users. Therefore, computers are not only the source, but should be the focus of today's technology concerns. We are now faced with both the problems and the benefits of the microcomputer age.

Devices that were thought to be impractical to market or impossible to design several years ago are a reality today. From the control of children's games to the complex concepts of sophisticated industrial products, the microcomputer has made the seemingly unattainable commonplace. These changes are generating the challenges of today and the future in the area of service and diagnostics.

A Volatile Environment

The volatile technology environment influences the management of service through the frequency of change, and the seemingly immediate obsolescence of electronic devices, materials, and products. This is a result of the rapid acceleration experienced in the early phases of microelectronic development and application. Several barriers in manufacturing technology and component speed are being encountered that are causing the rates of change to decrease when compared to the rate of change experienced in the first decade of microelectronics. These barriers will likely be surpassed and the rate of acceleration will again increase. However, the barriers provide an opportunity to reflect on the strategies that must be developed to address the present and future servicing problems as the service requirements change to keep pace with computer technology advances.

The changes in microcomputer technology have occurred rapidly in the last decade. To a large degree, these changes have been driven by the demands for a micro device that provides features similar to available minicomputers. The expanded base of applications and the availability of improved software development equipment have made the microcomputer an economical means of controlling a large variety of products, from massive commercial equipment to everyday applications in the home.

Service Impact

The negative aspect of this evolutionary cycle we are specifically concerned with is its influence on many aspects of field service. Providing basic service for products containing microcomputers has had effects on training programs, the preparation and publication of service data, and the selection of test equipment, in addition to the stocking of service parts. The techniques used to cope with these changing service demands will determine a company's future success in the service of its products. Although the rate of change may be slowing, future changes in microelectronics are inevitable.

New Features and New Complexity

The computer advancements we have mentioned have increased the features a product can provide the consumer, but also have added enormous complexity to the job of the field engineer. The field engineer must now understand the mechanics, electronics, and computer aspects of a product's operation to be able to diagnose failures and repair the products. Of possibly even more importance, the ratio of product cost to product feature has changed dramatically.

To add additional pressure on the service organizations, the reduction in the cost of computers has allowed for substantial enhancement and growth in the features offered without a comparable increase in overall product cost. Therefore, maintaining an attractive ratio between product cost and the cost of service support is becoming more challenging.

Demands on the Field Engineer

The knowledge required and the responsibility of the field engineer today are considerably more extensive than those of several years ago. Although the basic requirements are the same (good product knowledge and an understanding of the customer's application of the product), the extent of specialized knowledge required to provide economical service has become nearly impossible to maintain by even the most skilled field engineer.

The servicing dilemma has resulted in many new and some revolutionary approaches to providing service. Some of these are based on the very technology that has caused the dilemma — the computer and the microcomputer. Using the computer to solve service problems in a computer system allows for great productivity gains. Actually, it makes the impossible possible. The need to cope with these new product technologies has driven many advances in servicing technology, and the demand for more advances continues.

Some Things Stay the Same

Customers still insist on reliable products — this has not changed from the earliest days of service. In today's competitive environment, the serviceability and maintainability of products are becoming increasingly important as customer dependency on computer-based products increases. At the same time, all of this must be accomplished in an economical fashion that does not add significantly to the cost of a product. As the cost per feature decreases, the cost of service, as a percentage of the product cost, tends to increase. This ratio must be managed for a manufacturer to remain competitive and to provide affordable products to satisfied customers.

3

Elements of the Product Life Cycle

In every phase of the product life cycle, customer satisfaction through ongoing service must be emphasized.

Design, manufacturing, and serviceability engineers seldom share the same views of the life cycle of a product. Their individual viewpoints are often centered around their involvement during a limited span within the product life cycle. This leads to decisions that have a tendency to benefit that particular period in the cycle, possibly at the expense of another period. The result may be a series of compromises having an overall negative influence on the economics or performance of the product when considering that life cycle.

A knowledge and awareness of the life cycle stages of a product are extremely important in developing an effective service strategy. Often decisions made early in the life cycle have a lasting impact on the cost and effectiveness of the service required during the longer term of the life cycle. Ongoing support and maintenance features may contribute greatly to the initial product manufacturing costs, but these steps taken early in the product life cycle to enhance long-term maintainability, will pay back for the entire service life cycle. A review of a typical product life cycle may provide some insight into the service considerations required at various points in the cycle.

Source of New Products

Most new products are the result of either a new need (opportunity) in a specific market or enhancements to a current product. Therefore, the new product is either intended to fulfill a requirement in a new consumer area or it provides additional features beyond existing products. Some new products are targeted at increasing the user's productivity. These are the type that demand the greatest service considerations and long-term support. When a customer is expecting productivity increases, the up time of the product, or the availability of the product, becomes more critical in the purchasing decision. The considerations that are given during the early stages of a product's life cycle will have dramatic effects on the eventual failure rates and service demand of the product.

There are three key elements that determine the service burden and, therefore, the product availability: serviceability, maintainability, and reliability. These will be explored in more detail later; here we will limit our focus to the elements of a product life cycle.

The Start of the Life Cycle

The product life cycle usually begins with a user-needs analysis. This may come about through the results of a market survey, or as a suggested innovation to provide a product not commonly or currently available. In other words, there is a market identified for a particular new product.

At this time, a product definition is developed to establish the basic operating criteria. This includes features, function, and product technology. Also at this point, it is important to define the basic service objectives, the diagnostic approach, and the service philosophy for the product. These will, it is hoped, support the up time and usage requirements of the customer in an economical manner. Usually, at this stage of the life cycle, the definition of service is somewhat broad and is not very specific as to the means to achieve the service objectives. Preparing this service definition is often considered a service planning function prior to the formal proposal and description of the new product.

The service definitions available would most likely be statements and assumptions regarding service goals, heavily based on customer need and the selected technology. Items such as the Mean Time Between Failures (MTBF), Mean Time to Repair (MTTR), and Mean Time to Diagnose (MTTD) would be defined in terms of maximum occurrences and maximum hours per service call. The means of accomplishing these goals are considerations in the later stages of the product life cycle. Thus, what is actually prepared is a description of what customers will consider an acceptable level of service.

The Design Stage

Once the product has been defined and the basic service philosophy established along with the market analysis, the next step in the life cycle is the actual design stage. This is when the entire future of the product will be determined. This includes the design for the successful and satisfactory operation of the product and the design to provide a reasonable profit from the sale of the product. The service features and servicing approaches determined at this stage will have a significant impact on future revenues.

The involvement of an engineer skilled in and devoted to serviceability techniques and applications is essential to service success at the design stage.

A design engineer prescribes methods to be used in making the product function as specified, while the serviceability engineer provides input regarding failure modes and determining cost-effective means of diagnosing and servicing the product.

The serviceability engineer's role is to define the diagnostic and repair procedures and to expand on the basic service philosophy so that the goals established for service will be met in a cost-effective manner throughout the life of the product. This effort will involve constant trade-offs with design criteria to arrive at a sound economical solution to predicted service requirements. The cost of the service features must be a compromise between initial product cost and longer term, ongoing service and maintenance costs.

Another time-consuming and often neglected responsibility of the serviceability engineer is the verification and testing of the specific diagnostic and service approaches. There needs to be a high level of confidence in the ability of the diagnostics to locate equipment malfunctions. The time required to verify both the diagnostic and servicing procedures to be certain they meet service design expectations can limit the amount of testing possible. Because of this, it is even more important that the serviceability engineer devise thorough verification procedures. Any temptation to check the diagnostics on paper alone should be avoided. A lack of diagnostic testing and verification may lead to an ineffective service support procedure when the diagnostics are used in actual field service situations.

Manufacturing Approval

Based on demonstrated performance of the engineering models or prototypes, the next stage of the life cycle starts after approval to manufacture has been granted. At this point, the responsibility for the product shifts to the manufacturing engineers.

It is crucial that the serviceability engineer stay closely involved and prevent manufacturing changes from adversely affecting service features. Also, this stage of the life cycle may be the final opportunity to incorporate additional servicing aids and techniques. A sensitivity to manufacturing changes must be maintained to hold to the service plan goals. Gains in service performance that were achieved during the design stage can be lost during the manufacturing stage if the serviceability engineer does not maintain contact with the project.

Other elements of the total service package that begin to become final at this time include the development of publications, training modules, and service documentation. It is necessary to plan these activities carefully to be fully prepared to support product launch and customer availability.

It may seem that the serviceability engineer has an active schedule during the design and manufacturing stages of the product's life cycle, but the major work still lies ahead. The service effort doesn't usually peak until sometime after product introduction.

Final Preparations

The next stage in the life cycle is generally short in duration but very active for the serviceability engineer. This is the time during which the final preparations are made prior to initial shipment of the product to customers. Service data and other necessary documentation must be produced and distributed. The product launch training for field service personnel is conducted, and the first use of the service procedures takes place. These initial training programs often provide the first feedback from the users regarding the diagnostic and service effectiveness. This feedback often results in more fine-tuning of the service and training programs, but it is usually too late to make major changes to the architecture or service philosophy. It is important that the engineers and training designers be prepared for this feedback and that they accept it constructively.

Customer Availability

Customer availability marks the time when returns begin to be realized from the company's investment in a new product. As the product is sold and distributed throughout the market, the support and maintenance phases of the equipment and service procedures begin. It is truly the longest stage of the life cycle. This can be three to five times as long as any of the previous stages.

The Extended Outlook

As critical as diagnostic and service design is during the design stage, diagnostic and service procedure maintenance is critical during the remaining stage of the product life cycle. Keeping the diagnostics current throughout the useful life of the product helps maintain the expected quality of service and the desired availability of the product to the customer. To accomplish this, the engineers in the service support area must keep the service procedures current as product improvements and modifications are made. Too often, the engineers who possess the greatest knowledge, skill, and expertise regarding a product are redirected to other new product starts. This usually occurs immediately following introduction and customer product availability. This resource allocation invites increased maintenance and service expense, with less customer satisfaction, since retraining and relearning are then continual for the engineering support staff.

Service Discontinuation

Eventually, the life cycle of a product comes to an end. It is now time to establish the historical records and documentation. Although support and production by the original manufacturer may end, the product will most likely be used continually by some customers. Other customers, however, may represent a new market segment, in that the product may now be affordable to smaller size businesses, while some original customers may still continue to receive a level of productivity from the product that satisfies their needs. In any case, service and parts support will still be required by some customers. Only when this transition step is completed will the product life cycle truly come to an end for the original manufacturer.

Product Life Cycle	Service Activities
Market for product is defined	Define product, establish basic service philosophy, define diagnostic approach, evaluate product technology and complexity.
Design and prototype stage	Design prototype, input serviceability features into design, refine diagnostics, complete service philosophy definition.
Approval to manufacture complete	Begin production, serviceability development, debug diagnostics, document service procedures, develop training modules.
Ship products to stock, build inventory	Move products to distribution, begin training, complete product trade trials, refine diagnostics, distribute documentation, implement feedback procedures.
Customer availability	Service equipment in field, update and maintain diagnostics, maintain documentation, incorporate modifications, evaluate feedback, conduct customer training.
Discontinue service by original manufacturer	Establish historical records and documentation, provide continued service support for remaining customer base, arrange for longer term parts support.

Summary

In the discussion of a product life cycle, several stages were described. Each stage, though often different in content, is equally important to a successful product support program. When planning for the events to support a product, emphasis should be placed uniformly on each aspect of the cycle. Extremely large amounts of up-front effort are not a substitute for a lack of adequate support later in the product's life cycle.

All too soon after product introduction, the service and diagnostic procedures begin to become outdated and, without adequate attention, begin to lose their effectiveness when engineering priorities are shifted to the next new product. The changes that take place in the experience of the field engineer may dictate revisions in the diagnostics and service procedures. The diagnostics and service procedures must be flexible enough to accommodate these anticipated changes.

4

An Approach to Service Design

All approaches to service design must support the service strategy while satisfying customer expectations.

The approach taken, and methods used, by a serviceability engineer to develop diagnostics and serviceability for a product are of utmost importance and will have a major impact on the quality of the service results achieved. In service design the primary objective is usually the same — to provide appropriate and effective means of isolating malfunctions and to repair the product. First, the product must be testable to the macro level, and then diagnosable at the functional level, and finally at the detailed level. However, the serviceability engineer is often tempted to begin developing the means to achieve this objective at the detailed level before the preliminary work is done. This often leads to a less-than-desirable or less-than-effective servicing package.

The Approach

The following steps outline a possible approach to determining the type of diagnostics and service features required for a new product. This approach is intended to be a logical guideline that will help an engineer begin to establish product diagnostic and serviceability requirements. In addressing a specific product, unique aspects of the product or the marketplace may dictate that additional items beyond those covered in this document be included in the preparation of the overall service philosophy and the overall approach to diagnostics.

In all cases, service-related inputs must be considered in a timely manner which correlates with design and manufacturing engineering time lines. The role played by each service group in establishing the service philosophy and implementing the service procedures is of prime importance to the service organization's success in supporting the product in the most cost-effective manner. Nearly every service area needs to provide critical data at the appropriate time in the product life cycle. Service planning, financial, technical, and parts supply organizations must all work in harmony to create a successful product introduction.

Getting started at the right time, in the right direction, with a sensitivity to the needs of all the units involved presents a difficult challenge when dealing with today's complex matrix of diagnostic and testability alternatives. Often, beginning the detailed diagnostic design for state-of-the-art architectures is a strong temptation for the serviceability engineer. Success will only be realized when the engineer forces himself or herself to maintain a vantage point where the entire product and marketplace can be viewed for establishing the goals and objectives of service and product support. The goals and objectives must address the needs of *both* the product and the marketplace.

The First Step

At this point in the development of a new product, a definition of the product exists (maybe only a functional definition) and a target marketplace has been identified.

The servicing goals and objectives for product support need to be established. These include the targets for the length of service calls and number (frequency) of service calls that are acceptable to the customer and generally experienced in the marketplace when dealing with similar equipment. Consideration should be given to the level of customer involvement anticipated in the servicing of the product. The basic objective here is to be sensitive to company interests and remain competitive with the product offering. We do not want service costs to discourage product sales and, at the same time, we want to establish realistic servicing goals and service demand estimates.

When the first step is completed, the following should be available:

- A functional definition of the product.
- A service philosophy defining field service personnel involvement and customer involvement.
- The product technology and relative design complexity analysis.

It is extremely important to note that the actual diagnostic and servicing methods have not been established. This decision process is a method of achieving the goals and objectives set forward at this point, but it is not a portion of this step.

The Second Step

At this point, a set of service objectives or goals that meet the needs of all areas involved exist, and the functional complexity of the product is generally understood by the engineers. In taking the second step in the design of service, the following must be accomplished:

- The service engineers need to create a list of alternative diagnostic and service procedures for the product. The exact application of these procedures is most likely unknown at this time, but the procedures may be reviewed for their contribution in meeting the service objectives and goals established earlier.

- Design engineering must begin to formulate the basic design of the engineering model or prototype. Actual product design may or may not be closely following the functional model outlined previously. It is important that the serviceability engineer monitor these design modifications to keep the diagnostic and service recommendations current with the product.

- When the second step nears completion, a prioritized list of servicing alternatives and diagnostic approaches needs to be created by the serviceability engineer and agreed to by the design engineer. These approaches will allow for the service objectives and goals to be met. The effect of some of these diagnostic routines may not be as economically sound as desired, and trade-offs may be necessary. The extent of this trade-off process will vary on a product-to-product basis.

- A typical list of diagnostic approaches may include several of the following: the need for special test equipment, test points, and feedback circuits; use of telemaintenance by the field engineer or customer; on-board diagnostics and prompting error messages available to the field engineer; special applications of centralized support; and placement of performance indicators.

- A list of service considerations may include: board replacement versus component repair, accessibility of mechanical subassemblies or components, preventive maintenance performed by the field engineer and/or customer, historically troublesome parts, and reliability considerations.

It is of utmost importance that at the end of this step everyone realize that the "how to" and the actual application of the service design has not begun. What has taken place is that alternatives have been reviewed, estimates have been made with recommendations for how to accomplish the service objectives, and goals have been set for the product.

The Third Step

Now it is time to begin engineering the applications of the serviceability and diagnostic approaches selected to meet the service objectives. This includes the following:

- The serviceability and design engineers should develop the most cost-effective application for the diagnostic and servicing approaches selected. Although trade-offs and changes will occur, modifications to the diagnostic application cannot compromise the basic diagnostic and service objectives. Changes at this point in the overall servicing strategy may force many other company units to modify their product implementation tactics.

- Not only should the serviceability engineer consider the application of service and diagnostic technologies to the product, but, possibly more important, he or she should address the use of these techniques by the end users. In other words, *what are we going to do with the application of this technology to enhance product servicing?*

With the completion of this step, the application of the diagnostic and service procedures to meet the objectives has been decided. It is now known how the service objectives are going to be met and it is time to begin the detailed engineering step.

The Final Step

At this point, the necessary plans and procedures have been reviewed. Detailed application to the product to achieve the desired results can now proceed in a straightforward manner. The serviceability engineer now needs to address the electronic and mechanical details of the product functions and begin the design of detailed diagnostic and service procedures.

Other Areas

Although only some of the service design and development criteria were addressed, the activities in the remaining areas are of no less importance to the product's success. The systems that support field service need to be in place, an adequate supply of spare parts needs to be provided, service personnel and customer training must be developed, and, possibly most important, field personnel need to be committed to making the chosen diagnostic and service procedures work.

The Point of the Approach

A great deal of up-front work must be done to be successful in establishing the service philosophy and service procedures for any given product. If the diagnostic design is started before a sound servicing philosophy is established, the service objectives will be lost.

It is possible to attain nearly any service goal. Regardless of how great the amount of customer involvement, or how infrequent the service occurrences need to be, or how short the call duration, these objectives can be met — at a price. This price of service leads to frequent trade-offs. These trade-offs can be reduced to a minimum if adequate attention is given during the early planning stages to the servicing needs of a product. A sound service program can only be achieved by careful and diligent planning during the early stages of product design and development.

5

Serviceability and Reliability

Reliable products simply wear out rather than fail to meet customer expectations during their useful life.

Two of the key elements in controlling the actual field service burden of a product are serviceability and reliability. These two elements have a direct influence on the equipment's availability to the customer. Before beginning a discussion of serviceability and reliability, the relationship of the two terms must be established.

Serviceability Is

Serviceability can be defined as the result of the process during equipment design that influences the economy of the performance of maintenance. This maintenance may be performed by a field engineer or the customer. By keeping both the field engineer and the customer in mind when addressing serviceability issues and objectives, the impact of the serviceability design can be even greater on the overall costs of service and, therefore, profitability of the product.

Reliability Is

Reliability can be defined as the result of the process during equipment design that determines the frequency of equipment malfunction or failure. In current products, the reliability extends from the mechanical assemblies to electronic parts and to the software associated with the product. A malfunction by any one of the product components can create a loss of product availability.

Serviceability and Reliability Together

The relationship between reliability and serviceability can be understood best by thinking of reliability as the determining factor in how often service will be required, and serviceability as the determining factor in how long it will take to isolate the problem and make the necessary repairs. This can also be stated as the MTBF being controlled by reliability and the MTTR being primarily influenced by serviceability design and serviceability features. As an example, the product diagnostics are considered serviceability features since they have a direct impact on the MTTR.

Toward More Reliable Products

Increasing influence is being placed on the reliability of products. This is illustrated by the changing view of the importance of service by many large corporations. Such vehicles as quality circles, reliability groups, and many other intracompany programs are addressing the issues of quality and reliability of products.

Actually, these efforts are primarily reliability improvement and manufacturing improvement efforts. The importance of these efforts should not be understated, since they directly influence the product failure rates. If there were no failures there would be no need for serviceability or for the service industry. However, even though it may not be possible to eliminate failures, it is practical to produce equipment or products containing a high degree of reliability. However, in products and systems where reliability measures are extreme, failures still occur.

The companion element which addresses these failures when they occur is serviceability. The importance of this design issue (serviceability) is often given much less attention than is given to the importance of the reliability of the product.

The Role of Serviceability

Serviceability in the design stage will influence the economy of maintenance, to paraphrase our definition. This will have a significant effect on the cost of service, and eventually the cost and profitability of the product. However, service procedures that produce the maximum availability of the product to the customer, such as board exchange, may drive the service costs to unacceptable levels.

Serviceability was also defined as strongly influencing the MTTR. This expands the definition of serviceability to include two primary areas or elements of service — the time to find the cause of a problem or malfunction and the time to repair the problem. Estimates made on the relationship between these two times indicate that the diagnostic time (the time to find the cause) may be up to 70 percent of the total time of the service call. The time to repair a problem may only be 30 percent of the total time of the service call. These estimates are based on the service of complex, computer-based products and may not apply to some less complex, highly mechanical products or areas of products.

Because it is not practical to design and manufacture failure-proof products, serviceability, or the increasing ability to provide service, presents a great opportunity to equipment manufacturers. Unfortunately, the role of serviceability and the science of serviceability are not fully understood, or adequately addressed in many industries.

Everyone has probably experienced cases of poor serviceability. Classic examples exist in all industries, but may be more prominent or visible in the automobile industry. Finding the fuse block in some cars becomes a challenge in itself, while more extensive repairs require special tools and massive disassembly. This leads to longer repair times and customer frustration with the product. Sometimes manufacturing costs and assembly costs exclude good serviceability from the final product design. These service decisions, however, should be based on the economics of the product life cycle and not on immediate, short-term manufacturing benefits. It is therefore essential that a serviceability engineer be part of the design team *and* the manufacturing team to make sure that the proper service considerations are made.

Serviceability as a Science

The science of serviceability engineering encompasses many design considerations that are targeted toward reducing fault isolation times and actual repair times. Several elements of this science include: testability, maintainability, accessibility, diagnosability, repairability, and, of course, the ability to determine that the product is functioning properly. A qualified serviceability engineer must understand many aspects of product design and the product marketplace to be successful, since, as stated earlier, serviceability features are usually incorporated as the result of service objectives (which are met by economic trade-offs against manufacturing and design considerations).

The Serviceability Engineer

The services of a serviceability engineer are crucial to incorporating well-structured serviceability into new products. Generally, a serviceability engineer will have an educational background of either mechanical or electrical engineering. This is only the beginning of the knowledge required to be effective as a serviceability engineer. The aspects of serviceability from this starting point have to be learned on the job, within the industry, and based on the experiences of the engineer and the individual job.

Such seemingly straightforward issues as what previous training the field engineer has and what tools he or she has and is capable of using can dramatically affect the success of many serviceability measures applied to a product. This can be learned only through practical experience.

Serviceability Aspects

An engineer assigned to address the serviceability aspects of a new or existing product must consider many product and market characteristics. An indication of the complexity of this assignment is shown by the considerations that follow. Some of the issues that require the attention of the serviceability engineer are:

- Accessibility of replaceable and repairable components and assemblies.
- Tolerance requirements and complexity of electrical and mechanical adjustments.
- Preventive maintenance requirements.
- Positive detection of both intermittent and continuous malfunctions.
- Amount of disassembly required for repair.
- Steps needed to verify the correction of the malfunction.
- Steps needed to verify the total system operation.
- Potential for customer-created service calls.
- Possible elimination of field engineer calls.
- Possible ambiguity of messages or instructions.
- Historically troublesome parts and subassemblies.
- Functional approaches to the diagnosis of the mechanics and electronics.
- Standardization (all aspects).
- Interaction of adjustments.
- Possible involvement of the customer in repair and maintenance.
- Support of diagnostics using system software.

- Self-testing capabilities of the products.
- Environment of the marketplace (domestic/ international).
- Commonality of parts and components.
- Need for specialized tools, skills, and training.
- Logical sequence of diagnostic and repair tasks.
- Potential for incorrect assembly, installation, or repair.
- Awkward, tedious, or dangerous diagnostic/repair procedures or situations.

This list is only a general description of the product-related aspects considered part of the job of a serviceability engineer. Each item could be expanded to identify more exacting tasks and considerations.

Summary

Reliability and serviceability are the topics of many articles and books. The importance of both of these items in determining the cost or burden of field service should not be underestimated. Product failures and the time to repair them directly affect product costs and profits. The overall costs of service will be reduced as a result of the current emphasis on product quality (reliability) by many industries today. However, an equal opportunity for savings and productivity exists through the application of good serviceability measures during product design. Not only do we want a product that is reliable, but we also want a product that is economically diagnosable and repairable to provide the customer maximum product availability.

6

Laboratory versus Field Service Testing Equipment

A properly equipped field engineer will increase customer confidence and satisfaction.

The market for specialized test and measurement equipment used by field service organizations is often overlooked and frequently misunderstood by test equipment manufacturers. The test equipment needs of a field engineer are significantly different from the needs of a laboratory technician or design engineer.

Test equipment is needed by the field engineer to isolate problems in products and confirm the repair of electronic and computer-based products as efficiently as possible. A field engineer uses test equipment in day-to-day activities to determine how well a product is functioning and where failures, if any, have occurred. This need must be recognized as different from the needs of the design engineer, manufacturing engineer, and serviceability engineer. The field engineer is often working under direct customer pressure to diagnose and repair a malfunctioning product. The primary objective is to isolate the failure and repair it in the shortest possible time. The field engineer is more concerned with the verification of specified operating parameters than with developing the operating parameters as in the design areas. Therefore, precision of the equipment for service purposes may not have to be as great as for design applications.

Today's products include mechanical, electrical, and software sections which work together to make a product perform its intended function. Each section is usually designed and developed by an individual design engineer (computer scientist, mechanical engineer, or electrical engineer). Generally, in a complex product, one engineer will not be an expert in the other product areas. The level of expertise in these other areas will be enough only to allow that engineer to complete the assignment and contribute to the product design.

The field engineer is faced with a different need, which is to evaluate the entire product — electrical and mechanical sections, and software. This broad and more general responsibility generates a different need for test equipment and measuring instruments.

Test Equipment Training

Another factor forcing a reevaluation of the test equipment supplied to field engineers is the amount of training required to operate this equipment as it is applied to a specific product or specific area of a product. Because the field engineer is responsible for many different products, or models of a product, it may be impractical to provide the person with the in-depth training needed to understand in detail the product and all its functions. The analytical capabilities and documentation required to diagnose complex products using laboratory-type test equipment increases the training burden significantly.

A Solution?

Fortunately, intelligent test equipment is becoming available for field service. This equipment addresses the needs of the field engineer and the unique requirements of field testing. Intelligent test equipment requires training and accompanying documentation, but at a much lower level than laboratory-type instrumentation. At first, this appears to be an ideal solution to the problem of field testing, but the development of the required diagnostic and repair intelligence in test equipment may equal the development effort required for the product itself.

Considerations

When making the determination regarding the specific type of field service instrumentation needed, several items must be considered. Cost is always a consideration, but there are several considerations over and above cost that determine the skill level required by the field engineer in using the equipment, listed as follows:

- The service philosophy for the product (i.e., circuit board replacement versus component level repair).
- The targeted service call duration.

- The long-term support required for the test equipment.
- The application of this test equipment to other products which the field engineer repairs or will repair in the future.
- The ability of the intelligent field service equipment to adapt to advances in technology.

The considerations mentioned above are only some of the items that determine the feasibility of using this equipment to support a product. The acceptance of this equipment by the field engineer is of equal, or maybe even greater, importance.

There is no single piece of test equipment that will address the many needs of the various service tasks. This is not to say that as many functions as possible should be combined into one device. Without a goal of minimizing the number of test devices required by a field engineer, the number and types of distinct service test devices would soon become unmanageable and would require large cars or trucks to transport them from customer to customer.

In the remainder of this section, the basic considerations for all types of field test equipment, not the specifics of that equipment's function, will be reviewed. The specifics of the function of a particular piece of test equipment are too closely related to a particular need, and therefore, any judgment about these applications must be addresssed at the individual product level. The following apply if the requirement is for signature analysis, logic analysis, current measurement, or whatever other parameter must be evaluated by the field engineer in the field environment.

More Considerations

First and foremost, the test equipment must be as small and as lightweight as possible. This is critical in the use of test equipment for on-site customer service and for the acceptance of the equipment by field engineers. A size and weight that present no problems in the engineering laboratory can be unusable in the field environment. Just imagine carrying a laboratory-type oscilloscope up and down flights of stairs from one customer to another. After one trip, the need for the field test equipment to be as small and light as possible is easily remembered.

A second important requirement for field service test equipment is that it be rugged and designed for the extreme conditions in the field. The equipment does not reside in a uniformly heated or cooled laboratory. Temperature, humidity, pressure changes (due to altitude variations), and vibration extremes are common. From the cold of a northern winter day to the heat of the summer in the South, the equipment must be able to survive and function properly. If the equipment is not rugged enough, the field engineer will soon lose confidence in its operation and resort to alternative, less cost-effective means of fault isolation, generally "shotgunning" the problem using large quantities of parts and circuit boards.

Ease of use is as important as equipment size, weight, and ruggedness. Experienced engineers, working in a laboratory, are not confused when making complex measurements after multiple interactive dial adjustments. However, because of the large variety of measurements made by the field engineer, and the less frequent use of sophisticated test equipment in any given mode, confusion often results. This can lead to the incorrect diagnosis of problems, and increasing frustration for the field engineer with the test equipment. The key is to select field test equipment that is easy to operate. This includes the ease of connecting the equipment to the product under test. A simple edge connection or a clip-type connector not only saves valuable service hours, but helps in making the proper signal connections and the correct test equipment to product interface.

Another consideration in selecting field test equipment is the output it provides. There are two possible "outputs" from test equipment. The first is generally experienced in the laboratory environment. This output may be a series of software hexadecimal values, a trace on an oscilloscope, the value of voltage or current, or some other nonanalyzed data. This may be considered raw data. In order to determine the quality of the product operation, an analysis in some depth is required. This analysis is error prone and time consuming in the field service situation.

The second possible output can be referred to as analyzed or processed data. This output is specific to the results of a test and an analysis of these results. The intelligence is built into the test equipment; the analysis is not left up to each individual field engineer. The advantages of presenting analyzed data are realized in all areas of service from the training and publications area to the productivity of the field engineer diagnosing problems at the customer's location. Frequently, the more sophisticated test equipment can be used to determine what the proper "analyzed" data should be.

Finally, in addition to the considerations already discussed, there are many other requirements that need to be addressed when selecting test equipment for field use. Briefly, some of these considerations are:

the availability of repair for the test equipment, the amount and frequency of calibration required, and the necessary steps in validating the proper operation of the test equipment.

Trends

There is a trend toward the use of intelligent test equipment in the field. This type of test equipment provides troubleshooting capabilities for complex products that are relatively easy for the field engineer to learn and implement effectively. Unfortunately, another less visible situation that intelligent equipment creates was mentioned earlier, and that is a heavier development burden on the service engineering departments.

Most likely, an intelligent test tool is driven by software. Creating this diagnostic software adds a new dimension to the development of service support materials for a new or existing product. Without proper manpower allocation for the design and programming of these diagnostic routines, the task may become impossible to complete or the results may be less than satisfactory. The key element in increasing the manpower need is the verification of the diagnostic routines. This intelligent method of diagnosing equipment requires a more detailed analysis by the serviceability engineer of the failure modes of the target product and a testing of these modes in their predicted failure conditions.

Summary

Laboratory test equipment does not generally address the needs of field service in a practical manner. It is often too bulky, too complex to operate, too sensitive to environmental extremes, and requires exceptional analytical skills to interpret the output. The proliferation of many pieces of test equipment with very specialized applications creates not only a burden to transport from site to site, but soon becomes an economic problem.

Future field service test equipment designs are addressing these problems by incorporating software-programmable devices to perform complex service and equipment failure analysis quickly and easily. As one problem is being solved, a distinct and new one is being created — how to develop and maintain the diagnostic software required to power intelligent field-service equipment.

7

Producing Quality Service While Remaining Competitive

Quality value-added service is one of the few remaining opportunities to achieve the competitive edge.

A critical element when establishing a productive and cost-effective manufacturing organization is efficient product design. The importance of designing to meet the objectives of the individual product, while avoiding unwanted or "nice to have" features is well understood by all units of the design and manufacturing areas.

Efficiency is possible only because there are design specifications and performance guidelines. These documents specify what is and what is not required. Everyone contributing to the effort can test the design and manufacturing activities against these guidelines and determine the appropriateness of each and every action in meeting the goals set for the product. These controls are needed as much for the diagnostic design team as they are for the equipment designers.

Service Objectives and Philosophies

The service specifications referred to are the service objectives and philosophies. When they are available, many serviceability engineers read them and understand that they specify the goals that should be adhered to in diagnostic and serviceability design. Applying service and diagnostic technologies to meet goals without including enhancements that far exceed the goals is another matter entirely. Product history may indicate that the customer will assume the service responsibilities after the warranty period. This may dictate that more emphasis be placed on the short-term reliability and the long-term serviceability. That is, for the short term, the product should be as reliable as possible to control service demand, and, in the long term, the serviceability features should make customer diagnosis and repair possible.

The design and performance specifications never state that the product should perform as many functions as possible or include as many features as possible. Likewise, there is rarely a service objective that states only that the product must be made as serviceable as possible. Unfortunately, the service objectives are usually not as specific as the design specifications, but in most cases give guidelines which indicate the desired service (diagnostic and repair) costs and methods that are considered acceptable for the marketplace while protecting the desired profit margins. However, success of meeting service specifications can only be measured and determined after the fact.

Designing to Meet Service Objectives

Service objectives, which are carefully developed using evaluative data, have specific goals that should be adhered to. A serviceability engineer may be tempted to exceed the goals of the service objectives and further reduce the average diagnostic and repair times in an attempt to reduce service costs. However, the total effect of this enhanced serviceability may be the opposite of what the engineer intended, actually increasing the overall service costs.

Service objectives not only support the efficient diagnosis and repair of a product, but they must also support the cost-effectiveness of the service of a product. Serviceability enhancements that exceed the objectives for diagnostics and repair may influence the overall costs of support in ways that are not readily apparent to the service engineer.

The following example describes enhanced serviceability for a power supply. The example illustrates how the enhanced serviceability features affect the total cost of providing service.

Example

Let us imagine that the service objectives for a new product include a diagnostic and repair time forecast of one hour in 80 percent of the service calls. This goal states that the time required to locate the problem and the time to repair and verify the fault should not exceed one hour. The serviceability engineer will develop the diagnostic and repair procedures for a straightforward power supply. To achieve the objective, the service call must be completed in one hour. Also, we'll assume that the power supply is not a field repairable assembly, but is simply replaced in the product.

Armed with the service objective, the serviceability engineer begins to develop diagnostic and serviceability procedures to support failures in the power supply. Probably the first thing that comes to mind is to include a visual indicator that the power supply is operating. LEDs are fairly standard devices for such a task, and they are inexpensive and easily interpreted. If the LED is off, the supply is suspect. This will save diagnostic time for each power supply failure.

In order to make voltage readings on the supply more easily, the serviceability engineer includes test jacks for voltage measurement. The operation of the supply is easily diagnosed with the jacks. First, look at the LED. If it is on, the supply is probably good; if not, use the test jacks to read the voltages and determine if they are correct. Finally, repair the supply problem by replacing the supply, if necessary. The time to diagnose the problem and verify the cause is estimated by the serviceability engineer to be approximately 10 minutes.

To make the replacement of the power supply as serviceable as possible, the serviceability engineer includes a quick-disconnecting cable assembly and easily removed fasteners which secure the power supply in the product. Field engineers can now replace the failed power supply very efficiently. The estimated time to replace the supply has been established by the serviceability engineer at about 10 minutes.

The total diagnostic and repair time has been designed to require 20 minutes for failures in this power supply. This does not include the time required to obtain the necessary parts. Adding the indicators for diagnostics and the serviceability features to reduce repair times makes this service call for a power-supply failure well within the one hour objective. But is this a real benefit to the product's productivity and profitability? *Maybe not.*

The Results

The technology applied to the diagnosis and repair of the power supply results in an estimated call duration of 20 minutes. This will probably not be the real-life call duration experienced in actual field service of the power supply.

If the service call cannot be eliminated through advanced service technology or through customer involvement in service, the call will have a minimum call duration. The minimum call duration is created by several elements beyond the control of service technology. These elements include: travel time to the customer's location, customer relations time (the time required to discuss the problem with the customer before and after the diagnosis and repair), and the time required to verify proper equipment operation before leaving the customer's site. Service procedures should be designed with these elements in mind.

A brief review of what unneeded diagnostics and serviceability features can mean in excess costs and personnel underscores how a service organization can grow unnecessarily. Several contributors to this growth are: the extra serviceability design efforts, design and manufacturing engineering time, the additional parts to be stocked and inventoried, and finally, the published procedures required to diagnose faults and to repair the power supply will be just as lengthy as if standard, less extensive procedures were followed without using the LED, test points, quick connectors, and fasteners.

Is Serviceability a Benefit?

Do we really benefit from this serviceability? We could be driving up the cost of doing business by requiring more engineers to design the service aid into the product, additional engineers for serviceability, assemblers to do the initial assembly, parts-handling personnel to inventory the parts, computer resources to track the extra components, personnel to inspect incoming parts, publication personnel to prepare documentation, and finally, managers to manage all these extra people! This is a lot of overhead for a service aid with questionable benefits.

The point is that we should design only diagnostic and serviceability aids that are absolutely necessary to meet the service objectives, and aids that will be used frequently by the field service personnel. Approaches need to be developed for those service incidents that match the frequency of occurrence.

Life Cycle Costs — Again

Attention is often given to the ever-more-popular term *life cycle cost analysis*. This life cycle is usually limited to the time period during which the product is actually being manufactured. Serviceability engineers base many cost justifications on the benefits received during the entire life of a product, compared to the initial design costs. In many situations, this is an excellent approach to identifying the effects of serviceability and diagnostic design. But when considering life cycle costs, the service life cycle (which may extend for years beyond manufacture dates) needs the greatest attention, not the often confused manufacturing life cycle. The service life cycle is that which addresses such factors as the skill level of the field service personnel, the product volume in place that requires either warranty or maintenance service, and the actual useful life of the product.

Superimposed on the life cycle is the learning curve of the field engineers. The steeper the learning curve, the less need there is for extensive diagnostics. In any case, diagnostics are only worth the investment if they are used throughout the service life cycle. Serviceability is worth the investment only if actual reductions in service time are needed to achieve the service objectives and service goals.

Summary

The key element in maintaining productivity in service design, and at the same time providing adequate serviceability and diagnostics, is excellence in service planning and service management. Service objectives must be uniquely designed to consider all elements of the service philosophy and strategy. The competition and marketplace must be thoroughly analyzed in order to be certain that the goals of the service organization are realistic. More time should be spent defining the service requirements rather than guessing what is needed to diagnose equipment.

Finally, good serviceability and diagnostic implementation must be identified as meeting the objectives in a cost-effective manner that returns benefits to the company and the customer when all elements of the service life cycle are considered. If the service call cannot be eliminated, it must be approached realistically. The proper service development procedure is critical to producing quality service while remaining competitive.

8

Productivity Opportunities in Field Service

Productivity gains in field service will result from the application of technology to the field service business.

Productivity improvements are often talked about, rarely understood, occasionally recognized when they occur, and are a predominant topic in the goal-setting sessions of most managers today. Some corporate "buzz words" come and go, but one which seems to endure is *productivity*.

A Measure

As a concept, productivity is a measure of the output of, or the results achieved by, a given number of contributors. Therefore, a productivity gain is realized when the same amount of output or the same results are achieved by fewer contributors. Also, a productivity gain can be viewed as an increase in output or results by the same number of contributors. Therefore, if productivity gains can be identified, a formula can be applied to measure these gains.

$$\frac{\text{Output}}{\text{Input}} = \text{Productivity}$$

How innocent this formula appears to be for something as volatile as the issue of corporate service productivity.

When considering productivity in field service, it is important to maintain a constant level of service support for a product. That is, the same quality of service must be delivered while operating within the same service philosophy. Variations in service quality will make

40

productivity impossible to measure. From testing and evaluating the operating parameters of equipment to the methods of repair, all aspects of service support for the product must be constant. Having an understanding of the parameters of productivity, let's examine several productivity opportunities in field service.

Definition of Field Service

If a measure of productivity in field service is to be made, it is necessary to keep in mind the definition of field service. To paraphrase our earlier definition, field service is understood to be the performance of preventive maintenance and corrective maintenance to make sure that a product operates in the environment it was designed for, to specification, and for its intended lifetime.

Good Parts Treated as Bad Parts

With data to support that more than 50 percent of electronics modules returned from the field will test as error-free, it is clear that opportunities to increase productivity must exist in the performance of field service and in identifying faulty components or assemblies. The overall effect of this large volume of good parts being replaced extends far beyond the parts themselves. The effect spreads to all areas of a company — from product design to manufacturing, to the marketing and pricing groups, and finally to the field service organization.

Imagine the inventory reductions possible if a significant number of these "faulty" components could be eliminated through improved serviceability and better diagnostic technology. When we refer to inventory, the entire parts-stocking scheme needs to be considered — from the supplies carried by the field engineer, to the local area stocks, to the central company warehousing facilities. Both the stocked inventory and the size of the pipeline will grow with an increase in demand for replacement parts. It is important to expend the up-front resources necessary to minimize the number of good components, parts, and assemblies replaced in the field.

The Pipeline

Beyond improved serviceability measures and diagnostic improvements, the total impact of good product in the replacement parts pipeline and the assembly pipeline can be reduced by taking measures to shorten the pipeline, or to get the good parts out of the pipeline as close to the source of entry as possible. Several test equipment manufacturers are offering reasonably priced, bench-top test equipment that can help reduce these pipelines. Strategically placed, these bench-top units are capable of identifying and sometimes assisting in the repair of electronic modules about to enter the pipeline. Identifying components that are faulty early on will eliminate a massive inventory buildup. Typical pipelines to support the products of major equipment manufacturers can be from three to six months long. This translates into three to six months of extra parts inventory. Reducing this pipeline can have dramatic effects on operating costs.

Intelligent Testing

A second approach to reducing the costs of providing service for complex products is to provide intelligent test equipment, which can be used to isolate failures in sophisticated products using the same field engineers currently in the field organization. The shorter development times for products using microcomputers, as compared to largely mechanical products, results in many generations of a product in the field at the same time. This fact in itself is a cause of confusion to the field engineer when trying to diagnose a failure. Training the field engineer to understand the intricate aspects of all of these products is impractical, if not impossible. The result will be that the field engineer need only be an expert in the use of the intelligent test equipment and not every product.

There are several positive and negative aspects to the development of intelligent test equipment. The initial investment is not trivial! Just to equip and support the field engineer with this equipment may be too extreme a financial burden for many companies. The source of this lies not in the advantages of this equipment, but in the limited number of different products this equipment can support at the time of its introduction.

The return on investment in this equipment will be realized in the future, and *only* if the company has a firm commitment to the success of this method of service throughout a product line or several product lines. All innovative approaches suffer from growing pains, which must be anticipated and accepted. The commitment is more of a business operating decision than a pure economic decision. That means that there is risk involved. As in many cases, the greater the reward, the greater the risk required. To achieve productivity gains, the gain is, in many instances, directly related to the amount of risk taken.

Equipment Complexity

Another problem intelligent test equipment can address in field service is the increasing length of time required to diagnose today's complex equipment using "traditional" tools and techniques. Maintaining this diagnostic time at reasonable levels will keep the call duration at an acceptable level. On-board or in-product diagnostics, computer-assisted test equipment, and sound serviceability features all reduce the diagnostic burden of the service call.

Features, functions, and enhanced modes of operation are multiplying in new products. These are the selling points of new products — the competitive edge. They are also one source of the lengthening service call duration. In all aspects of a service call — from the time a field engineer first discusses a problem with the customer, to the time required to diagnose the problem, to the time required to verify proper machine operation — the increased number of features and functions adds to the length of the service call. The application of intelligent test equipment can help in this area by eliminating certain functional areas of a product as the source of a failure.

Manual Testing versus Automatic Testing

In Chapter 1, an analogy of manual calculations to the speed of a computer was reviewed. The same analogy applies to manual testing versus the computerized testing of a product. In order to accurately perform the necessary diagnostic tests that the microcomputer can perform in several minutes, the field engineer would spend days completing these tests manually. A point of interest here is that at some point in time, the computerized tests must be developed step-by-step and verified for proper operation. This requires an extreme amount of time and effort. Remember that what the computer can execute in seconds requires days or years if done manually — this also applies to the diagnostic verification process. This really means that computerized testing methods require long development times.

Concentrating on the Customer

The ultimate productivity gain in field service is not realized by reducing the call duration or reducing the parts and inventory required, but rather it is realized by eliminating the call *entirely*. If this could be accomplished in all cases, there would be no field service organization required; realistically, eliminating all service is impossible. However, opportunities are arising from several technologies that can eliminate some service calls. This requires the application of technologies to increase customer involvement in the maintenance and repair of the equipment.

Customer training is a necessary means of allowing the customer to better understand the product. Many times a customer prefers to carry out repair without calling a field engineer. This provides the customer with maximum equipment utilization by reducing downtime.

Several new technologies provide an increase in the level of customer involvement in the service of the equipment. The intelligent test equipment reviewed earlier has the potential to increase the involvement of the customer in service; another technology, telemaintenance, can also be implemented to decrease field engineer demand by increasing the involvement of the customer.

Telemaintenance

Since telemaintenance can be developed following several approaches, its final implemented format can take many forms. Rather than attempt to detail all possible telemaintenance configurations, a brief review of some approaches follows, with added detail in other chapters of this book.

The common element of all telemaintenance approaches is the application of telecommunications to the service of a product. From this point on, the variations are extensive. The exact application and the modes of operation vary from manufacturer to manufacturer and product to product.

Assistance via communication channels may be in the form of access to an engineering staff. This concept is used extensively to support products used in the home and commercial products requiring complex, interactive adjustments.

A resource center is generally staffed by product experts to talk the customer through the fault isolation and repair procedures. Standard person-to-person telephone conversations represent the most basic form of telemaintenance. An opportunity exists in this telemaintenance configuration, as in several others, to include telemarketing during the service call.

Remote Diagnostics

More complex forms of telemaintenance are sometimes referred to as remote diagnostics or remote assistance. Remote diagnostics is the ability to maintain a diagnostic data base remote from the product. Telecommunications used to send diagnostics (primarily software and sometimes procedural routines) to the product under test at a remote location and to transmit the results of these tests to a central facility to be evaluated. This is the key to remote diagnostics, that is, the diagnosis is performed remotely from the equipment site. Possible benefits include the reduced demand for built-in diagnostics in each product and the ability to more efficiently maintain the one central diagnostic data base with current diagnostic data. The shortcomings of remote diagnostics are caused by the relatively slow transmission speed available over standard telephone lines and the protocols necessary to safeguard the accuracy of transmitted data. The use of communication protocols results in data being transferred over the telephone lines that do not aid in the actual diagnostic process but are used to secure the integrity of the transmitted data.

A final consideration and corporate benefit of remote diagnostics is the added security for proprietary diagnostic software and diagnostic technologies. This allows for simple restriction of access to the diagnostics of qualified and authorized field engineers.

Remote Assistance

Remote assistance is another form of telemaintenance. The difference between remote assistance and remote diagnostics is primarily in the physical location of the diagnostic and service routines. Rather than being located in a central computer, the routines are resident in each product. This minimizes the amount of data that must be transferred over the telephone lines and the problems of slow transmission speeds. The benefits of remote assistance, beyond the reduced telephone transmission burden, include the ability to exercise the routines on-site as well as remotely. This expands the number of variations of customer involvement possible in completing the service call. For example, some tests could be accomplished on-site with no additional assistance, while others would be controlled remotely.

Summary

There are many opportunities for productivity improvements in field service. Several of the opportunities with the most impact include the reduction of parts inventory and shortened pipelines through improved serviceability and diagnostic procedures, the application of distributed bench-top test equipment to shorten and "cleanse" the pipeline of good parts, the use of intelligent test equipment to reduce the skill levels and time required to diagnose and repair complex products, and increased customer involvement to minimize the number of service calls required by applying technologies such as telemaintenance to the support of products. As has been stated, the elimination of a service call is the ultimate in reducing call duration and service costs. This can, of course, be accomplished to some extent by increased equipment reliability. However, when failures do occur, there are opportunities to decrease the direct economic impact of these failures.

9

Field Repair via Component or Circuit Board Replacement

Carefully review any service philosophy to make sure that its impact on the field service specialist and the customer is positive.

Renewed interest continually surfaces in component level diagnosis and repair as an improved field service method replacing the more popular circuit board replacement service philosophy. One proposal is that component replacement would be possible and more easily accomplished if all integrated circuits were socketed. This would permit the field engineer to readily exchange the integrated circuit at the equipment location and reduce the need for costly spare circuit boards.

Before committing to such a servicing philosophy, several critical issues must be considered. Even though there appear to be cost-effective reasons for instituting component level repair, the actual impact of this service philosophy needs to be fully understood in the context of its influence on the total servicing costs.

Providing cost-effective service that meets the expectations of the customer and, at the same time, provides an acceptable return to the company, requires the development of the most effective service philosophy by the serviceability engineer, as well as diligence in adhering to that philosophy by the field engineer.

Some of the issues that require consideration are discussed in the following sections. Each of these issues must be considered separately for specific impact, and all issues must be reviewed together to achieve the objective of providing high quality, cost-effective service. This is not intended to disqualify component repair as a cost-effective solution to repairing circuit failures in field locations. It is important to remember that neither method is always right. There are circumstances that sway the final decision in either direction.

Diagnostic Design

The design of the diagnostics to support the service of a product needs to be comprehensive to the level of service defined by the service philosophy. When circuit board replacement is the chosen method of repair, the diagnostics should be designed to isolate failures only to that level. If the service philosophy indicates component level repair, the design of the diagnostics must isolate problems to the component level.

The costs associated with the design and maintenance of the diagnostic routines will be compatible with the level of diagnostics required to support the service philosophy. Component level routines can be costly when compared to diagnostic routines that isolate failures to the circuit board level. This cost can be ongoing as equipment modifications affect the actual components used during the manufacturing process.

The higher cost associated with diagnostic design for component level service can be offset through reductions in parts cost, equipment downtime, return call frequency, and circuit board exchange and repair expenses. These issues need to be addressed while the serviceability engineer is determining the most effective service philosophy for the product.

Publications

The publications required for a field engineer to complete the necessary service vary, based on the service philosophy. If component level repair is indicated, the components must be identified and described to a level of detail that will allow the field engineer to understand the function of each component in the circuit. Random substitution of *seemingly* identical components can be avoided only through a listing of equivalent integrated circuits approved by a design engineer. Since each component requires a unique part number, the parts list could be extensive.

Electrostatic Discharge

As technology advances, the complexity within individual components increases. One result of this is a greater number of functions performed by every component. Component manufacturers are making this possible through sophisticated techniques of miniaturization. A service problem that is caused by this miniaturization is the susceptibility of these devices to electrostatic discharge (ESD). Many times the damage caused by ESD is not "terminal," but does cause a degradation that may result in intermittent failures. The handling of the components by the field engineer, the packaging for shipment by the parts center, and the transportation of the components must be rigidly controlled to make sure that good parts are available to the field engineer to repair the product.

Parts Stocking and Distribution

If component repair techniques could completely replace the need for circuit board assemblies, the impact in the area of parts stocking and distribution would be minimized. Unfortunately, the need for circuit boards would still exist to some degree. The components might then represent incremental parts and part numbers.

An added concern for the parts-stocking centers will be the cross-referencing required as several manufacturers offer the same or similar components. Many circuits are so sensitive that substitute parts cannot be used. This means that exact replacements will be necessary to safeguard product performance. In any case, locally available integrated circuits should not be used since their reliability is always in question, and the data required for the field engineer to determine which ones are suitable replacements will seldom be available.

Field Service

The perceived quality of service and the professionalism demonstrated by the field engineer are important for establishing customer confidence. The methods used to diagnose and repair sophisticated products have a strong impact on how the customer views the quality of service and the quality of the company.

Following a service philosophy of component level repair requires that the field engineer disassemble more of the product at the customer's site. For some product areas this would not be a problem, but in the case of many products, the environment at the customer's site is not ideal for this type of service.

Another consideration when planning for component level diagnosis and repair is the test equipment that will be required to evaluate the operation of the integrated circuits on any complex circuit board. If the diagnosis is to be done in a manner that isolates problems to the chip level, on-board diagnostics will probably need support from additional test equipment. The service impact of this equipment is discussed in a separate section, but providing service to the component level requires the field service specialist to carry additional test equipment and tools.

Finally, diagnosis and repair to the component level generally require additional time for the field engineer to complete each call. The result is that more field engineers may be needed to support the existing product base. This added expense must then be traded off against the anticipated savings in circuit board inventories. An analysis of the economics should be carefully undertaken to make certain that any change in service philosophy is beneficial. The implementation of component level repair will have a dramatic impact on the way the field engineer conducts the typical service call.

Reliability

Equipment reliability directly influences the frequency of product failures. Reports regarding component level repair all indicate that the reliability of circuit boards that use socketed integrated circuits is reduced. This creates a greater demand for service.

One way the reliability is affected is in the use of sockets for the components that are field-replaceable. As sockets are soldered onto the circuit board, the reliability losses associated with the insertion of the integrated circuits occur. This happens regardless of whether the insertion is done using automatic equipment, manually during manufacture, or manually by the field engineer. Data describing the decreased reliability have been published which indicate that the losses are directly related to the number of socket pin connections.

Another reliability consideration is the possible problems caused during circuit replacement in the field location. It is often difficult to determine if an integrated circuit has been inserted properly. For example, a leg of an integrated circuit may be bent over, making intermittent contact. This could generate an unnecessary return call or could create an incorrect diagnosis of the fault. That is, when replacing the suspected integrated circuit fails to correct the problem, the field engineer may not know if the indicated repair was correct, or if the problem still exists because some other component is causing the malfunction. The result is generally a lower certainty of correct repair and in no way reflects on the skill level of the individual field engineer.

Manufacturing

Providing for expedient component level repair by field engineers adds to the cost of manufacturing printed circuit boards. The extra costs incurred may be justified when either the circuit board inventories or the field repair times can be demonstrated to be less. Unfortunately, this is seldom the case except in special circumstances.

Manufacturing costs that could be easily identified include the cost of the sockets for the integrated circuits (quality sockets often cost more than the circuits themselves), the cost of inserting the integrated circuits into the sockets, and the added costs for testing the printed circuit boards. With today's technology, automatic insertion equipment greatly reduces circuit board assembly costs. In order to include sockets on the circuit board, manual insertion of the integrated circuits is sometimes necessary. This requires extra handling and extra labor to complete the assembly process.

As a final step in the manufacturing process, the circuit boards are completely tested for functionality. These tests are conducted on sophisticated equipment that cannot only determine circuit and component failures, but also isolate assembly errors. Sockets add many additional points of potential failure. An integrated circuit may not be seated properly, or a leg may have been bent during insertion. Also, the socket itself may be faulty. All of these potential problems equate to greater manufacturing costs.

Test Equipment

If the service philosophy is to be component level replacement, and the diagnostics are to support this method, the field engineer must have adequate test equipment available to identify failures to the component level. This will require test equipment beyond that which is commonly used in the field today.

The additional test equipment creates a number of different problems. The most visible problem is the cost of this equipment. Since the on-board diagnostics can only be effective where adequate feedback is available, all remaining circuitry without feedback must be evaluated using equipment such as logic analyzers, signature analyzers, logic pens, and oscilloscopes. Some of this test equipment is commonly found in the electronics laboratory, but not in the field environment.

The only alternative to this test equipment is to replace several integrated circuits when the diagnostics can isolate a problem only to an area of a circuit board. This method has proven to be error-prone and costly. When a failure cannot be traced to a specific integrated circuit, employing methods of "shotgunning" the problem often injects new problems that previously did not exist. At the very least, the actual cause of the failure will never be known.

Total Cost

When considering the total cost of changing a service philosophy to component level repair, the total cost may be more than a total of the individual costs. The additional costs will include the cost of doing field repair following two separate diagnoses. It is not practical to abandon a current board replacement philosophy entirely at a specific point in time. In practice, the transition is a gradual process.

Each and every printed circuit board should be reviewed to determine the application of component repair to that board. In several cases this will be more complex than a pure technical review. As an example, the cost of the circuit board may be driven by a single integrated circuit on that board. An A-to-D converter component may represent the major cost of the board and replacing this component may cost more, or be as expensive as replacing the entire board. Other similar situations occur when the complexity of the adjustments required to recalibrate the circuit board exceed the capabilities of the test equipment available to the field engineer.

The major objective of service organizations is to provide high quality, cost-effective service. All service philosophies need to seek this objective, and a critical element in reaching this objective is the total cost of the chosen service procedure throughout the life of the product.

Training

Field engineers who are expected to diagnose and repair printed circuit boards to component level need to be trained to accomplish this task. Regardless of the individual skill proficiencies of any field engineer, all field engineers must be able to complete the required steps to diagnose and repair a given failure.

Diagnostics that provide component level isolation are more complex by their very nature. The number of fault isolation steps is greater than those required to isolate failures to the board level. The complexity of these steps to find the faulty component is also greater. In order to understand the diagnostic procedures, and at the same time maintain diagnostic development costs at realistic levels, additional training will be required.

Once the faulty component has been diagnosed, component replacement is necessary. Since these components are more sensitive than the circuit boards to handle, the field engineer must be made aware of proper integrated circuit handling procedures. This also requires training beyond what is usually available. For the repair or replacement of integrated circuits that are not socketed, the field engineer needs to be skilled in the proper soldering techniques that provide good circuit operation and minimize damage to the integrated circuits. Without these special skills, component replacement is not an effective servicing technique.

Components that Should Be Socketed

There are some components that should be socketed for either field replacement or for centralized circuit board testing. The number of such components, however, is quite small when compared to the total number of integrated circuits used on all the printed circuit boards.

If a component has been identified as one which has a high failure rate, it should be a candidate to socket. This will help to reduce the printed circuit board pipeline by affecting the board repair at the equipment location. It will also permit the field engineer to diagnose problems associated with the specific circuit board more thoroughly.

Components that are programmable devices should also be considered for socketing. Software modifications may require frequent exchanges of these integrated circuits to keep the product performance at optimal levels. The socketing of these integrated circuits will definitely reduce the circuit board inventory requirements.

A third classification of components that should be socketed is the components that must be removed for automatic circuit board testing in the manufacturing and centralized repair area. The time required to remove and replace these components without socketing justifies the added expense for the sockets.

Impact of Surface Mount Technology on Field Service

The circuit boards of the late 1980s will be assembled using a technology commonly referred to as surface mount technology. To understand all of the implications of this change in manufacturing technology on field service is far beyond the scope of this section, but a new approach to servicing printed circuits in the field environment will be required.

Surface mount technology may prohibit the field repair of all printed circuit boards. Simply stated, an integrated circuit will be attached to the board without inserting the legs of the integrated circuit through the board. Surface mounting is just what the name implies — the components, including the discrete components and the integrated circuits, are attached to the board with adhesive compounds and aligned with the circuit traces. The board is then soldered to complete the circuit connections.

There are many productivity advantages to this assembly technique in the manufacturing process and, for this reason, surface mounting is gaining in popularity. Surface mounting also allows for dramatic increases in the density of components per square inch of board by making boards with components on both sides possible. These circuit boards will provide a new set of challenges for field service organizations.

Summary

For specific situations, providing sockets and all the associated service features that allow component level repair to be done routinely by the field service engineer is an attractive alternative service philosophy to the more common circuit board level of service. However, there are many considerations that must be addressed to make sure that the highest quality and most cost-effective service methodology has been chosen. In addition, the most practical method of implementing component level replacement is to design this capability into the product.

10

LAN Diagnostics and Service

Network diagnostics and service require special attention by all company areas, for it is in networks that the parent company can quickly lose its identity.

An understanding of Local Area Network (LAN) technology is necessary to prepare for the service challenges LANs will create for any company that connects a product to such a network. An overview of a typical LAN configuration will establish a base of knowledge as to the elements that comprise an LAN.

An LAN is a means for computers within a small geographic area (usually a single building) to communicate with each other. The transmission data rates are moderately high, usually one million to 20 million bits per second (1 to 20 Mbs). The LAN may be comprised of one or more CPU, mass storage (tape, disk, optical disk) devices, gateways, and user terminals. LANs are a relatively new development and little is known about the failure modes that may occur. But it is known that a failure in one piece of equipment may cause the entire LAN to fail. When one considers the large numbers of products that may be connected to the LAN, it is easy to see that there are many ways that an LAN could fail.

ETHERNET* Network

The ETHERNET Network is one variety of an LAN. The complexity of such a network can best be understood through a description of what makes up such a network.

ETHERNET uses a coaxial cable to transmit data at a rate of 10 million bits per second (10 Mbs) on the network. A maximum of 1024 nodes can be connected to the network. A node has the interface and control circuitry to communicate on the LAN. Generally, the node

---

*ETHERNET is a registered trademark of Xerox Corporation

has some type of CPU. The maximum distance between any two nodes on the network is 1500 meters.

Nodes are attached to the network through a transceiver. The transceivers may be placed on line by severing the coaxial cable and attaching to the transceiver, or by using a network cable tap. The tap arrangement allows the transmitter to be connected or disconnected without affecting the continuity of the cable.

In order to coordinate data flow within a network, a set of data handling rules is established. This set of rules is referred to as the access protocol. The ETHERNET Network uses Carrier Sense Multiple Access with Collision Detection (CSMA/CD) as an access protocol. CSMA/CD works much like a verbal conversation among several people. For example, anyone may speak or listen (multiple access) to anyone else. When someone wants to speak, he or she waits for silence (carrier sense). When there is a silent period, the person may speak while the others listen. Sometimes two or more people start to speak at the same time and cause interference (collision). This collision is detected and each person is then assigned a back-off time before being allowed to start to speak again. ETHERNET nodes use a random back-off time so that the same nodes do not again start to transmit at the same time.

Definitions

Several terms are used commonly in discussing LAN. The definitions of these terms are included to help in understanding this technology.

- *Coax Segment.* A coaxial cable, terminated at each end, with characteristic impedance.
- *Link Segment.* A point-to-point link terminated at each end with a repeater set. Maximum propagation delay end-to-end is 2750 nanoseconds. No other stations may be attached to a link segment.
- *Reflection.* The return of signal energy caused by a change in impedance of the transmission media.
- *Repeater.* A device used to retransmit data to other coax segments.

ETHERNET Verification

The ETHERNET cable is the backbone of the entire system. All communications between nodes occur on this cable. Proper installation of this cable and the attached transceivers is a necessity for proper network operation. Verification is a time-consuming process, but the time spent in verification will save time in diagnosing network problems after installation.

Verification begins prior to network installation. Installation plans should be reviewed for completeness, accuracy, and standards compliance. Specifically, the following items should be checked:

1. Adequate number of nodes in network.

2. Adequate number of nodes (including repeaters) per coax segment.

3. Adequate length of coax segment. Whenever possible, the coax segment should be made from a single cable length. If it is necessary to build up a coax segment from sections, the following procedures should be used in order of preference:

   • Use cable sections from the same manufacturer and lot.
   • Use standard sections of cable if cable sections from the same manufacturer and lot cannot be used. This will minimize signal reflection in the cable caused by discontinuities in characteristic impedance.

4. Adequate length of link segment. Propagation delay rather than distance is specified, since other media (such as optical fiber) may be used.

5. Adequate transmission distance between any two nodes.

6. Adequate length of transceiver drop cable. This cable should be made from a single section.

7. Minimum coax bend radius. This is one to watch for, especially with a floor conduit. A tighter bend may change the characteristic impedance of the cable, causing signal reflections.

8. Coaxial cable grounding. The shield conductor of each coax segment should maintain an effective electrical contact with earth reference. This requirement safeguards a good signal reference. This grounding should take place at one point only. Grounding at a single point ensures that there are no stray currents flowing through the shield conductor of the coaxial cable. It is recommended that the contact with ground be

made using the electrical service grounding electrode. Connection may be made directly or via a conduit. All connectors should be insulated to avoid a second unintentional grounding point.

9. Transceiver placement. To minimize signal reflections, the coaxial cable is marked for placement of transceivers.

10. Coaxial cable type. PVC cable cannot be used in environmental air space. An example of environmental air space is the space above a suspended ceiling which is used as an air return in an air conditioning system. This restriction is to protect personnel from the toxic vapors released if there is a fire. FEP (Teflon) cable should be used in environmental airspace.

Items 1 through 9 deal with physical constraints of the ETHERNET Network. Failure to comply with these constraints will adversely affect network performance.

Verification of coaxial cable installation should be carried out immediately after installation (prior to transceiver installation). As a last resort, the coaxial cable installation verification can be performed at the same time as the transceiver installation verification. The use of a printed checklist is highly encouraged. This checklist and all other data should be placed with the site documents and become a permanent part of the maintenance record. The person performing the inspection should check for adherence to the site plans, with special emphasis placed on the items mentioned previously. The following checks should also be carried out:

1. Visual inspection. Terminators and connectors properly installed, tightened, and electrically isolated from possible ground paths (building frame, water pipes, etc). Coax has sufficient support, no tight bends, and no visible damage. Coax should be separated from power conductors.

2. Grounding. Check that each coax segment is grounded at one point only. This can be done using a multimeter and a clamp-on ammeter.

3. Shorts and continuity test. A digital multimeter may be used for this test. However, a Time Domain Reflectometer (TDR) is a much better tool for this purpose. A TDR sends pulses down a cable and looks for pulse reflections. The pulse and the returning reflections are displayed on the CRT of the

instrument. Shorts and opens can be located by using the distance calibration on the TDR. On some models, the accuracy is greater than 0.5 feet. By contrast, a multimeter can only locate a fault to the cable section. Some TDRs have a plotter as an option. This feature may well be worth the extra cost. All plots should be placed with the site documents or maintenance files. The use of a TDR is a necessity in the following conditions:

- Long cable runs.

- A large number of transceivers installed.

- When nonstandard cable sections have been used to build a coax segment.

The installation of transceivers should be verified prior to network operation. The following items should be covered:

1. Visual inspection. Transceivers should be placed on bands marked on the coax. Check connection of drop cable to transceiver. Check installation of drop cables.

2. Shorts and continuity test. Using a digital multimeter or TDR, perform shorts and continuity test of coaxial cable.

3. Test operation of transceivers. A portable transceiver tester should be used.

Following network verification, make sure that all documents and TDR plots are placed with the site documents. It may be desirable to have copies of these documents also stored at a central location.

Network verification does not end when the network begins operation. Verification of the network should be redone if the network configuration is changed (the addition or removal of coaxial cable sections, or the addition of transceivers). Intermittent network crashes or other failures are another reason for performing a network verification. In short, if there is a question about network operation, perform these verification procedures.

Power Verification

As LANs become more common in product installations, the quality of the line power serving these networks also requires verification. The assurance of power quality may be as critical to network performance as the quality of the network installation. Improper wiring in just one piece of equipment can cause a number of problems, ranging from personnel hazard to network disruption. Voltage sags, surges, spikes, dropouts, brownouts, and blackouts may cause loss of data, network crashes, and failure of components. Worse yet, these power problems might not be readily diagnosed as such. As the power problem continues, the frustration level of the customer and field engineer will rise as numerous service calls and part replacements fail to correct the problem. At this point, a product exchange may occur. When the new product exhibits similar problems, the customer may replace the current vendor's equipment with that of another vendor.

It is important that AC distribution and power quality be verified prior to installation of the network. This will eliminate some probable causes of equipment failure right from the start. The use of a printed checklist is encouraged. Findings of the power verification survey should be placed with the site documents.

Equipment is available for verifying power line distribution and power quality. Errors in wiring can be checked by instrumentation such as power distribution testers. All receptacles serving equipment should be checked using these tools. Additionally, power scopes are available for monitoring power quality. If power quality is suspect, a power monitor should be placed on-site for a minimum of one week. There is no way to predict what effect power problems will have on personnel safety or equipment reliability. If any problems with power distribution or quality are discovered, the installation of equipment should be postponed until corrections are made and verified.

One last warning—never assume that power is not the cause of problems, even after initial verification. If a service exchange of equipment is a prospect, check the power prior to the exchange. Also check the power if there is a rash of board failures, intermittent system crashes, or other mysterious events.

Summary

In this section, we have attempted to outline some procedures that should reduce the number of network failures. It is important that the installation of a network be done right the first time. Verification procedures are one step in this process. Equally important is the need for well-written site specifications. The site specifications should be understood by sales personnel, field engineers, installers, and, most importantly, the customer. Only when proper network verification is completed will the reliability of installed networks improve.

11

Data Communications Service

Servicing the data communications in a product or using data communications technologies can be the bane and boon of a service organization.

A vast array of products being serviced today rely on complex data communications to function at perfection. These products include various types of LANs as well as complex communications between on-board processors performing various functions. In addition, remote diagnostics are fast becoming a requirement for the cost-effective repair of complex equipment. With this increase in product complexity, service organizations must continue to try to provide the expertise, training, and tools to accurately diagnose and repair data communications problems.

Training Is Needed

A goal in this pursuit is to provide adequate training for the field engineers. Training is essential because of the current emphasis on data communications, both in remote diagnostics and in complex multivendor networks. A lack of training can cause even routine, easily solved communications problems to become frustrating, seemingly unsolvable service nightmares. Data communications problems can cost a great deal of money and cause customers excessive downtime. Also, given the lack of industry standards for data transmission, customers who connect equipment to an existing network in an unusual or unanticipated fashion can create hard-to-pin-down, intermittent hardware and software problems.

An Example of the Problem

Even the RS-232C Standard, well-recognized and commonly used for data communications, can be an enormous source of problems when performing even the most simple control functions. In addition to the 25 pins and various control signals available, there are also voltage levels, length of cables, event timing, and the effects of the controlling hardware and software to be considered. Even the slightest modification can create confusion or cause intermittent product failure.

In a typical example of a data communications problem, a major equipment vendor's printer was to be connected over a phone line to another major vendor's minicomputer, using two statistical multiplexers. The printer would not function properly and would constantly overflow its data buffer. This obviously pointed to a lack of flow control on the part of the printer, or a refusal of the computer to accept the method of flow control used by the printer.

Actually, the problem was both of these items plus the fact that the statistical multiplexers were not transmitting the proper control signals. It turned out that the printer would not use the protocol that was common to the rest of the equipment. Instead, the printer was configured with one of the RS-232 pins to signal a buffer full condition. Since the pin used is generally unassigned in most RS-232 applications, the cable did not have a wire for that pin. Furthermore, the statistical multiplexers would not transmit this control signal, and if they did, the computer would not recognize the signal as a flow control signal. So much for the RS-232 "standard." To solve the problem, the control signal from the printer had to be connected to a pin that the statistical multiplexers would transmit.

This, however, was not the end of the problems because, on the other end of the phone line, the computer would not recognize the transmitted signal as a flow-control from the device. Therefore, another wiring change had to be made on the computer end of the communications path. This usually simple installation of a printer, connected in a fashion not anticipated by the manufacturer, took two engineers experienced in RS-232 configurations a full day to complete. Furthermore, if the proper tools and training had not been provided, the problem would have been more costly to correct.

This is only an example of problems that will need to be addressed if service organizations are to continue to provide the type of leading edge service that customers have come to expect. Consistency of design and a combination of on-board diagnostics, training of the field engineers, and accurate and extensive publications will be needed if quality service is to be provided in the data communications environment.

Communication Tool Box

To deal with data communications failures, proper tools must be provided to the field engineers. Of course, these tools must be lightweight and easily used to be practical. Easily used, in this case, means that once the skill is learned, it can be recalled with little or no lost time, even after several months of nonuse. Data communications problems will not be the most frequent service problems, especially on mechanically intensive equipment, but they are frequently the most difficult to diagnose and the most time consuming to correct. This is often because the two products involved may be at entirely different locations.

One tool for dealing with data communications failures is the breakout box. This tool is designed to examine interface problems found in RS-232 interface configurations. Options on some models include bit error-rate tests and test pins to alter the control signals (for example, to configure a null modem cable to connect between two terminals). A breakout box is essential when investigating the actual hardware of the RS-232 interface.

Another diagnostic tool that applies on a higher diagnostic level is the communications protocol analyzer. These instruments give the trained data communications expert an excellent means of viewing not only the interfacing requirements, but also the actual data that is traversing the communications line. With knowledge of the various protocols that are commonly used, a field engineer can quickly and accurately determine the problems in a communications environment. Protocol analyzers are being used extensively in both developing and diagnosing data communications hardware and software.

Keeping Up-to-Date

Advances in data communications are occurring daily, and it is important for service organizations to keep abreast of these advances for the service of complex communication products.

The advances in modem technology during the past few years have allowed new applications for remote diagnostics by increasing dial-up speed to 2400 bits per second and increasing reliability by adding error-correcting protocols into the firmware of the modems. Dial-up speed is now approaching the 9600-bit-per-second range for full-duplex, asynchronous communications. Advances such as these continue to improve the cost-effectiveness of remote diagnostics by decreasing the connect time needed to identify or correct problems. This cost-effectiveness is also realized because software changes and revisions may also be accomplished remotely.

Even further increases in data transmission can be expected through data compression techniques, which use the probability of certain characters appearing to decrease the overall size of text files. For example, in ASCII text files every character is represented by exactly 7 data bits. This means that the letter "E," which is very common, takes the same number of bits as the letter "Z," which is very uncommon. Some compression techniques use this fact in exactly the same way that it is used in the design of Morse code. That is, the common letters are assigned the fewest bits, while the uncommon letters are assigned more bits. In a scheme such as this the letter "E" may use only 2 bits, while a "Z" may be 16 or more bits. By using compression techniques, dramatic reductions can be made in the size of text files transmitted and therefore the effective speed is increased.

This method, however, is not practical for many program or data files because of the randomness of the transmitted characters. For transmitting such files as error logs, a custom compression technique could be developed to take advantage of the unique probabilities associated with a particular service organization's records. This would also address the problem of security within the data channel.

Reliance on Data Communications

All of the signs within the industry point to an increase in reliance on data communications. This is evident in the increase of dependence on LANs. With such communications—intensive applications becoming commonplace—service organizations should concentrate heavily on developing field engineers who are trained to apply the hardware and software necessary for this type of service environment. In addition to the growing volume of LANs, there are other service applications which rely heavily on data communications, and these are being applied extensively by service organizations to improve field service.

The Role of Remote Diagnostics

With the increasing competition in the service industries, remote diagnostics have been found to be a cost-effective alternative to the traditional field engineer dispatching technique. Also, some customers expect remote diagnostic capabilities to aid in keeping their critical machines on-line by producing quicker, more accurate solutions to problems.

Remote diagnostics allow the service engineer at a central location to interrogate an intelligent machine and determine the cause of a failure. Many times the problem can be corrected immediately by either the service engineer operating remotely, or the customer on-site. Other times, the field engineer can be dispatched to the customer site with the correct part and the correct knowledge to solve the problem quickly and efficiently. This capability benefits both the customer and the service organization.

To the customer, fewer service calls, quicker solutions to problems, and more up time are of primary concern. The service organization sees fewer trips to customer sites, and the quicker repair times translate into higher profits. But most important is the perceived quality of the service provided. However, this entire operation depends heavily on accurate data communication between the customer site and the service engineer at the central location. A breakdown in these data communications could mean not only a monetary loss, but also a perceived quality loss due to customer dissatisfaction with increased downtime. This loss could grow enormously if service engineers trained to handle data communications problems were not available to diagnose and correct the communication failures.

A more advanced form of remote diagnostics involves a call-on-failure feature. In this case, a complex product could detect a failure, call a service center, and have a field engineer dispatched to the location. This could all be done with no customer intervention, so that machines could be brought back to satisfactory working order before the customer realized there was a problem. This would represent an enormous quality edge over competitors for any service organization. A system of this type would require a sizeable design investment, but the entire scenario again would still depend on the accurate data communications between the product and the central service site.

Summary

Data communications is a complex and rapidly changing field. The benefits in cost savings and customer satisfaction are obvious. It is left to the individual service organizations to service the wide variety of communications-intensive equipment, and also to use data communications technology to further improve the cost-effectiveness of providing equipment service.

12

Field Service Training

Training is a key element in establishing an effective field service organization.

When discussing field service training, it is important to keep in mind that different types of training are required for field engineers and for serviceability engineers. The field engineers need training in operating, diagnosing, and repairing equipment. In addition, it is important that they have good sales and customer relations skills. Serviceability engineers require training in how to develop the service plan for a product. This includes setting service objectives, estimating service time and frequency (based on the product design), developing diagnostic techniques, and preparing the publications and training for the field engineer.

Field Engineer

Training requirements for the field engineer can be met in several ways. There is no one way that is right for all cases. The decision must be made based on the number of people who require training, the size of the installed equipment base, the number of locations where equipment will be installed, and the complexity of the equipment design.

One way to make sure that all of the people who need training receive it is to develop a self-teach program for the product. This has the advantage that a field engineer has training available when he or she needs it. The burden of scheduling the training resources is placed on the local area (there is no need to have centralized training rooms and instructors available for a "class"). In addition, travel expenses are minimized. The biggest disadvantage of this method is that there is very little hands-on time (especially with larger or more expensive products). Not only is the trainee deprived of some hands-on experience, but there is little opportunity for one-on-one interaction with a product expert.

If a self-teach program is determined to be the most cost-effective way to provide the required training, there are still several ways to present the material. Training media such as linear videotape or computer-controlled interactive video disk (which both delivers and manages the training) are popular delivery methods. Because trainees can actually see how service procedures are performed, these media are effective and efficient, since it is not necessary to have equipment present and travel expenses are diminished. Another method is to use a book or manual that presents the material and asks questions to determine the comprehension level.

Regional training classes are another method of providing training. This can be done either by having several trainers working simultaneously in each region (especially if a large number of people need training quickly) or by having the trainer travel to different locations. This method places some of the burden of travel on the trainers and should cost less overall (in travel expenses) than a central training location. As with the self-teach program, it is usually too expensive to have equipment at the training site. So, once again, the trainee would not get the hands-on experience that would make some of the service procedures clear. One big difference over the self-teach program is that the trainee would have an opportunity to interact with a product expert and other students, learning from their questions. Depending on the number of classes that have to be taught, there can be permanent training centers established, or space can be rented as needed.

The last training method that we will discuss for field engineers is completely centralized training. In this method, all of the people to be trained are brought to a central location. This is usually near the factory where the product is manufactured. The product experts (design, manufacturing, and service) are all relatively close to the training facility. This allows the trainer to draw on other people's expertise during the training sessions. It also facilitates feedback on equipment behavior, service procedures, and training methods more directly to their sources. In addition, if equipment is available at all, this method is usually the most cost-effective way to provide it for training classes. The biggest drawbacks of this method are the travel expenses and the expense of maintaining a permanent training facility (it is unlikely that space could be rented on an as-needed basis when equipment must be installed for the class).

The best way to determine the success of a training program is to measure the effectiveness of the field service force. Only knowledge of the training audience and evaluation of the expenses associated with the different training methods, combined with the market requirements, can determine which is the best approach in a particular situation. It can only be emphasized that there is no single approach that is correct for all situations.

Serviceability Engineers

How many colleges or universities can you name that have courses (let alone degree programs) dealing with serviceability engineering, service engineering, diagnostic engineering, or almost any other aspect of preparing to service a product in the field? In today's job marketplace almost all serviceability engineers are "home grown." That is, they develop their expertise through on-the-job training. The biggest problem with this type of training is that it takes a considerable amount of time to develop expertise in this manner. In addition, the sophistication of equipment and marketing competition today demands that service philosophies be implemented right the first time. There will not be a second chance for a product. This section will discuss the areas that a serviceability engineer needs to be familiar with to have the best chance of getting it right the first time.

Before getting into the technical aspects of a serviceability engineer's training, it is a good idea to discuss the general background a serviceability engineer should have. Communications skills are important in almost any job, but a serviceability engineer especially needs clear writing and good interpersonal communications skills. The writing skills are important in preparing the service publications that are to be used by the field force. The serviceability engineer must be good at organizing his or her thoughts and presenting knowledge on paper. From that point on, a technical writer can present the material. The serviceability engineer negotiates with design, manufacturing, and marketing to implement service features.

A serviceability engineer must also be able to plan the service development process. He or she has to be able to estimate how long it will take to develop, test, and document service procedures; develop and prepare the field engineer training program; and finally, to procure equipment for verifying procedures, taking pictures, making drawings, and training. The plan must also take into account the fact that by the time equipment is available, the service organization is in the critical path for delivery of the product to the customer.

Some of the job-specific skills required of a serviceability engineer include technology, knowledge of diagnostics or problem solving, service estimating, and familiarity with field operations.

Knowledge of the technology used in a product is critical in determining the service plan for that product. Without knowing how the product works, it is impossible to develop diagnostic and repair procedures. Estimating the number of failures and their frequency is also more difficult.

Diagnostic troubleshooting or problem-solving skills are perhaps the most important ones that a serviceability engineer can have. After all, the whole purpose of service is to solve problems and repair equipment. The importance of problem solving is well established in the home grown school of serviceability engineers. Typically, the most successful field engineers are promoted to be serviceability engineers. For the serviceability engineers without field experience, the problem-solving skills must be acquired on the job.

Service estimating is the process used by the serviceability engineer to determine the required level of service. By accurately estimating the number of failures for a given time period (MTBF) and the time required for diagnosing and repairing the failure, the serviceability engineer can determine if the service objectives for the product will be met. If not, he or she must then determine which area of the product is a candidate to reduce either the MTBF or the diagnostic and repair time.

Another aspect of service estimating that is often overlooked is response time. Part of the service objectives should specify what the average response time should be. The serviceability engineer should be able to use failure and repair data to determine the increase in service burden that will be placed on the field. This information can, in turn, be used to determine the number of field engineers required to meet the average response time requirement. Knowledge of the field service environment is also important in determining the service approach. The items that need to be considered include:

- What is the skill level of the field engineer?
- Does the person have a car to carry parts and service information?
- How many field engineers are available to service the product?

These factors will have a tremendous impact on the level of the diagnostics, the type and quantity of test equipment, the level of repair, and the amount of main office support required.

Summary

In order for any organization to be effective, its personnel must have the proper background. One of the best methods for acquiring this background is through training. Training should not be approached as a necessary evil, but rather as an investment in the future. In field service, there are many approaches possible for training. The most difficult part of training for field service is training new serviceability engineers. This may be best accomplished through on-the-job training and seminars.

13

Serviceable Software Is Not an Accident

If servicing hardware is not an easily demonstrated commodity, servicing software must seem magical to our customers.

Areas of this section will repeat several concepts discussed in more detail in earlier sections. They are reviewed here to provide reference to these issues as they affect the servicing of software.

Software Is a Part of Our Environment

The service problems that have come about since computer-driven and software-dependent products have become commonplace are forcing service managers to modify their approach to the provision of service for these new products. Almost every aspect of daily life is now influenced by the application of computers to help complete our tasks and by the software that controls these computers. Actually, computers and software have become a part of everyone's daily activities, and therefore are a part of our environment.

As our dependence on computer technology and the sophisticated software necessary to control it increases, our ability to perform critical functions effectively without the assistance of these machines is rapidly decreasing. Sometimes this dependence on computers leaves us essentially unable to complete necessary tasks when the computer system fails. For example, the dependence on the operation of a calculator to complete complex mathematical functions has left many, if not most, people incapable of completing these tasks when the calculator fails. Computer equipment failures are becoming operational crisis situations which demand the highest quality of service.

The Software Servicing Burden

The burden of delivering service for software-based products is shared by all areas of the service organization. To cope with the challenges in the area of servicing computer-based equipment, the problems must be addressed at the three primary stages of the product's life cycle. These stages are the equipment design stage, product introduction stage, and the customer utilization stage, which lasts throughout the remaining useful life of the product.

Service organizations have expended large amounts of resources to try to better address the problems created by the failure of a computer-controlled product, thereby reducing the service burden caused by these failures. Because the diagnostic portion of the service call usually takes the most time to complete, service organizations have expended considerable effort on comprehensive diagnostic procedures which locate the source of failures as quickly as possible. Some serviceability techniques have allowed field service personnel to readily isolate a software subfunction in the product as the likely source of an equipment fault. The approaches vary from sophisticated diagnostics in the product to telemaintenance routines that provide for the analysis of equipment failures from a remote location. Even such costly diagnostic procedures as circuit board exchange have been used to provide field service personnel a means of isolating the causes of equipment malfunction, which at an increasing rate may actually be failures in the product software, and not in the hardware.

Service Life Cycle Phases

To help gain an understanding of the problems encountered in servicing software-driven products, the product life cycle phases can be compared to service life cycle phases. The service life cycle phases that compare to the product life cycle phases are the serviceability phase, the service implementation phase, and finally, the service support phase.

Each phase of the service life cycle has characteristics that separate it from the others. Understanding the characteristics and considerations of each phase is of critical importance to the service manager if the level of service provided is to continually meet the customer's expectations. This section will concentrate on the initial phase of the life cycle, the serviceability phase, and with several considerations regarding service during this phase.

A Definition of Serviceability

The definition of serviceability that will be followed throughout this section is:

Serviceability is the result of decisions during system design that influence the economy of the performance of maintenance. This maintenance may be performed by service personnel, the customer, or by the intelligence in the product itself.

Software serviceability, therefore, can be considered as the focus of serviceability toward the software elements of the product.

Serviceability Objectives

During equipment design, when service engineers are developing service approaches for the electrical and mechanical portions of new products, serviceability is an ever-present engineering objective. With the goal of reducing the MTTR of a failure, design and service engineers have developed many innovative solutions to the challenges experienced in the diagnosis and repair of faults which can occur unpredictably throughout a new product.

If field service personnel are to continue providing the level of diagnosis and repair that will maintain expected equipment performance in computer-based products, the software and systems aspects of these products must receive equal attention during the equipment design phases. While the tools and techniques required for servicing software may be different from those used to isolate electrical and mechanical malfunctions, the primary objectives remain the same. These objectives can be summarized as those that reduce the time to diagnose failures and maintain the shortest possible repair times, thus resulting in maximum product use for the customer.

Serviceability, Reliability, and Availability

It is difficult to relate the contribution of serviceability to the success of a product without giving some attention to the two companion design disciplines of reliability and availability. *Reliability* is a measure of a system's resistance to failure. It can also be defined as the ability of a system to continue to operate in the environment for which it was designed. The term *availability* is defined as the probability that the system will work when it is needed. The availability of a system is, therefore, not to be confused with the system up time statistics.

In many applications, the statistical up time of a product is not nearly as important in practice as the availability of the product.

There are options during equipment design that provide easier access to, and repair of, failed components. Terms such as *accessibility, maintainability,* and *diagnosability* are frequently used when referring to hardware serviceability. When software entered the mainstream of product configuration, the science of serviceability design continued to focus on the electrical and mechanical portions of the product. This resulted in major controlling portions of a product which were neither serviceable nor maintainable by field service personnel, and which often generated much downtime when failures occurred.

Diagnostic Software

As described earlier, the MTTR a problem after an equipment failure is directly affected by the serviceability decisions made during the design of the product. Two elements that determine the MTTR are the time to diagnose a fault and the time to repair the fault once it has been isolated. In understanding software serviceability, the diagnosis of a failure will be a function of the diagnostic software and the diagnostic software tools.

Repair of the fault will be carried out within software service philosophies and procedures. Therefore, it is important to note that diagnostic software will be designated for the diagnosis of electrical and mechanical failures as well as software failures. The repair of the software will then follow different and distinct software servicing procedures when compared to hardware service philosophies.

Software Diagnostic Tools

Traditionally, service engineers have developed service techniques for the electrical and the mechanical sections of products using diagnostic procedures and diagnostic tools to standardize the diagnostic portion of the service call. In a similar fashion, the software service engineer will need to develop standard tools for the diagnosis of software failures. Since software is a different medium than hardware, the tools will also be quite different, but tools nonetheless.

It is important to focus on the fact that the field engineer who provides service for the software product will most likely be servicing several different software products during the normal work day. If the tools and the procedures used for the diagnostic process are not standardized, the result will be the same as if the diagnostic tools for hardware service support were not standardized—lower productivity and less effective isolation of product faults because of the lack of knowledge and familiarity regarding the application and use of these diagnostic tools.

Software diagnostic tools that have been used to improve the effectiveness of software maintenance personnel include tools of both the pure software and also tools in the instrumentation category. Tools in this category include a large variety of systems and software monitors and debuggers. Several examples follow.

The Watchdog Routine

One tool that can be used to diagnose software faults is the watchdog-timer routine. This routine is programmed to work in a manner such that when software failures occur, the timer will not generate its cyclic output at the proper interval. This will alert the system and the key operator to a possible failure. The value of such a diagnostic has been proven in software-dependent systems in sophisticated products which can fail internally while giving the appearance of proper operation. Thus, the watchdog timer can behave as the software analogue of an LED in hardware to help indicate subsystem failures. This routine is more closely aligned to a performance check than an actual diagnostic, since there is an indication that something is wrong, but no indication of what is causing the problem.

Trace Tables

Once it has been determined that a system problem exists, help in the analysis of that software fault can be made readily available through several diagnostics, which can be included in the design during the serviceability phase of product development. Trace tables, for example, are used to create a permanent record for the service person of the program flow on a disk, diskette, or other permanent storage medium. The service person can perform an analysis of the problem by reviewing the recent equipment events in the trace table. This may provide an indication of what was occurring when the failure happened, and thereby reduce diagnostic time.

Crash-Dump Analysis

When the software failure is more severe, a crash-dump analysis program may be required to evaluate the cause of the failure. This software diagnostic tool also needs to be designed into the product during the initial design stages. Although it may appear costly, it can be of great benefit to both the service and manufacturing groups. With the crash-dump analysis routine, a history of the program operation at the time of the crash and an analysis of the active tasks and devices will be readily available for the diagnostic session.

Trace Values

Maintaining a software trace value will provide additional diagnostic assistance when the software system fails. This value can tell the service person exactly what was happening when the crash occurred. The software trace value may give the clue necessary to determine the exact point reached in the sequence of operation when the system failed. Recovery from system failures can prove costly and lead to lengthy service calls. The trace value will help minimize this cost.

Other Software Diagnostic Tools

There are many other software diagnostic tools that can be used in addition to those already mentioned to assist field engineers in diagnosing system or software failures. A brief list of several of the more commonly used tools follows:

- Error history logs.
- File system analysis software (including Checksum and CRC programs) to detect corruption within static files.
- System monitors for multitasking system device status.
- On-line debuggers for the manipulation of memory and active or suspended task status tables.
- "Warm start-up" procedures for critical systems that are developed to save and store information crucial to the system software automatically.
- Telemaintenance for software and system analysis.

By designing software diagnostic tools into the product, the diagnostic time can be reduced to a minimum, and in some cases, these software diagnostic tools will be necessary to make even fault identification possible for field service personnel.

Instrumentation for Software Diagnostics

The diagnosis of a software fault may require the service person to use either instrumentation or tools more frequently associated with the servicing of the product hardware than the software. The list of hardware tools includes traditional digital test equipment such as meters, logic pens, and oscilloscopes, and more specialized test equipment such as logic analyzers and in-circuit emulators. Although traditional test equipment may seem to be of relatively little value in diagnosing software problems in products, it is of considerable value when working on the hardware-generated problems. (Remember, the software has to have some hardware on which to run.) The specialized test equipment, logic analyzers, and in-circuit emulators are of much more value when diagnosing purely software problems, but can also be of value in the diagnosis of hardware problems.

A consideration in the designation of tools in the hardware category is that they can be expensive. If any of the specialized tools are going to be used, they should be used on most, or as many as possible, of the products the person will service in a normal work day. The reasons for this are that the cost of the equipment itself, the cost of training the service person to use it, and the cost of the field engineer using the equipment (having to relearn how to use the tool each time it is needed) should be minimized. Without the manufacturer distributing the costs associated with this equipment across several products, their use could be economically prohibitive.

Side Benefits from Diagnostic Software

The diagnostic software goals developed during the design stage of a product can have dramatic effects on service issues beyond the MTTR portion of the service call. What may not be readily apparent is the influence of diagnostic software on the frequency of the service calls or the MTBF. When a problem is correctly diagnosed on the first call and the repair is thoroughly evaluated to ensure that the equipment is performing within specifications, the frequency of return or repeat service calls will be reduced to a minimum, and therefore, the MTBF will be improved. Any reduction in the number or frequency of equipment failures is an improvement in the economics of providing service. A significant reduction in the cost of providing service can be realized by reducing service frequency via better performance testing, where the "soon-to-be problems and failures" are discovered. After completing a repair, the field engineer will run a software-based performance test. The test will provide an indication of the overall health of the product. If some area is marginal in its performance, the field engineer will now be able to repair the problem before it becomes serious, or before it generates a new service call. Although the component reliability has not been improved, the frequency of failure has been reduced, with an accompanying increase in the MTBF.

Diagnostic software can also reduce the service-related burden of travel time. For example, the travel that may be necessary when a required part is not at the site can be avoided through the use of diagnostic technologies such as telemaintenance, which can be incorporated into the diagnostic software. This also allows initial, off-site fault analysis, which can point to the failed components before the field engineer leaves to visit the customer. Travel back to the local office for parts, or even for special test equipment, adds time to the service call and decreases the productivity of the field personnel.

Making Sure that the Diagnostic Tools Are Used

The cost savings possible from increasing the MTBF, reducing the MTTR, and the travel time required for a service call influence the economics of any service organization. However, the goal in implementing these service technologies is not to eliminate people's jobs or reduce their value to the company, but rather, to control service costs and to remain competitive in the marketplace. This is accomplished through the existing service organization being more productive by using improved diagnostics and repair procedures.

Service technology, largely supported by diagnostic software is, unfortunately, sometimes viewed as a threat to the field engineer and that individual's value as a part of the service organization. The software must not only be user-friendly, but the service automation it provides must not be a threat to the field engineer and his or her future value to the service organization. Therefore, when implementing these advanced service technologies, the impact on the skilled field engineer needs to be carefully considered.

Wherever possible, the user of the service technology should be included in the development and implementation of the new service approaches. This will give the service people ownership in the technology and allow for their participation in the change in their work environment. If this is ignored, the return realized from investment in diagnostic software will be minimized when tools are not used as effectively or as frequently as they were designed or intended to be used. The measure of success is not how well-designed the advanced service approaches are, but how well they are implemented and adhered to.

The Problems of Customized Software

As the hardware associated with computer technology is adapted to a wide variety of applications, the software is frequently modified (or customized) to a particular user's needs. The results of these special applications have positive aspects when considering the improved marketability of the product through increased performance and enhanced features, but can be negative when considering serviceability impacts (implementation and ongoing support for the equipment and the software).

Customized software can be as much of a problem to the service organization as is customized hardware. When the product is modified, the usefulness of the diagnostic tools can be decreased or destroyed. Sometimes, after the software is modified, just knowing how the product is designed to operate is a challenge. The importance of detailed, accurate documentation increases with the changes brought about through customization. To reduce the problems that are created when the original program is changed, field engineers must be able to identify a customized product, and guidelines should be in place to assist the field engineer in addressing failures in these products. Customized software is a prime candidate for remote assistance techniques. This allows the experts who have changed the software to help diagnose a problem in that software.

The Role of the Software Serviceability Engineer

In preparation for the development of a serviceable software product, the structure of the design and service organizations must be considered. In some organizations the design engineer has the additional responsibility for serviceability. This can lead to compromises in the approaches to the serviceability issues. The major objective of the design engineer is, traditionally, the delivery of a product on time, at a cost that is acceptable to the customer, and which provides an acceptable return on investment to the company. As in the case of serviceability for the hardware in a new product, adding serviceability into the software appears to make service objectives more difficult to obtain.

Any additional effort during the design stage of a product will surely add to the initial cost of that product. If only the design stage of the product's life cycle is considered in reviewing the economics, the added cost for serviceability features may appear to be excessive. Since most design engineers are focusing on the initial cost, serviceability becomes an unwelcome burden to the design effort. What is required is a focus on the total life cycle costs of a product. When these costs are included in the cost estimate, it soon becomes apparent that the long-term, higher support costs for a software product can eliminate any profit gains made by excluding the serviceability features during the software design stage.

Matching the Talent to the Assignment

To address the software serviceability issues, personnel who can concentrate exclusively on the diagnosis and repair procedures for the software portions of a product can be assigned to the product design team. These individuals will then interface with the design engineers as equal members on the design team. They are the software service engineers. Their contributions may have equal or greater influence on the total profitability of the final product, as do the contributions of the design engineer. Their software service procedures can achieve this by reducing the service and support costs throughout the entire life of the product. These costs include those of the manufacturing and the quality control phases.

The personnel assigned the responsibility of designing serviceability into the software portions of a product will face many nontechnical challenges similar to those faced by all serviceability engineers. There will be constant trade-offs with the design team, and these trade-offs will require extensive experience in prioritizing the severity of potential problems. Therefore, when personnel are selected for the position of software service engineer, the most experienced software engineers should be considered. Ideally, these people will also have actual exposure to the diagnosis and repair of software faults. This will help them to better understand what the field-service problems are, and what the most effective field diagnosis and repair procedures are to detect and correct them.

Improving Reliability Through Diagnostic Software

The staff of systems analysts and programmers can have a dramatic effect on the reliability and maintainability of the software they create. Several basic guidelines, if followed by everyone involved, will save valuable service hours for the entire useful life of the software. In addition, these guidelines will reduce the software maintenance burdens. These guidelines are known by every software development community, but are frequently ignored in practice, or are assigned low priority in the development stages.

Whenever possible, software should be designed to perform independent of any particular computer architecture. Software designed to operate in only one computer environment has a built-in vulnerability to advances in computer technology. With the technology of computers changing rapidly, the software that is specific to a single computer cannot be used on improved computer hardware. This flexibility may not always be possible to accomplish totally, but any movement towards less dependence on specific computer hardware will be a productive step.

Event Timing

In earlier days of computer development, it was common for event timing to be determined from the computer software processor cycles. This is still sometimes done in products where expense is the most critical factor, because this can eliminate the need for costly timing circuitry. If possible, it should be avoided, since it will bind the specific hardware and software together as tightly as possible. The goal of all software development should be to reach universal modularity in the design and programming of all products.

Structured Programming

The benefits of following structured design approaches in software cannot be overemphasized. Several companies offer excellent programs that detail this process of structured software design. Close adherence to the principles outlined in these programs will result in superior products that are understandable and maintainable by any software development engineer skilled in that structured design process. Without the structured approach, software can assume many personalities and become unmaintainable and difficult to understand.

Use of the Operating Program for Diagnostics

The maintenance of the diagnostic software is a source of extra expense which can be reduced through advanced design and planning. As the product control software is modified to add operational features, or to accommodate hardware changes, the diagnostic software is frequently affected, making it unusable. This is usually the result of separate, independent control routines being written to operate the various parts of the equipment only for diagnostic purposes.

An example of advanced design planning is making a software change in control routines and also in the diagnostic routines so that they will continue to monitor the performance of the product properly. In another case, the diagnostics can be made unusable in testing memory size and partitioning, if either of these elements is modified. One method of avoiding these problems is to use as many of the operational routines as possible from the product's control software as drivers for the diagnostic software. Thus, when control software is updated, the diagnostic software is also updated with little or no additional expense.

The Customer for Diagnostic Software

Unfortunately, the entire service problem is no longer limited to the strictly technical aspects of how to provide effective and economical service of a quality that will satisfy the needs of the users when dealing with software-controlled computer-based products. Service personnel are also facing an increasing base of sophisticated customers who are dealing with the precision and logical reasoning of their computer-controlled products on a day-to-day and hour-by-hour basis. This is creating an atmosphere in which customer demands are for near perfection in the operation of their equipment, and they are expecting a quality of service to support this level of performance.

The ways of doing business in servicing software-controlled products are very different in several aspects from the business of servicing products that are mainly hardware-based. However, the same basic principles apply. The service call contains the same elments. The product design phase contains the same stages. The manufacturing process has many of the same steps. The difference is the medium in which the product is created. Bits and bytes combined in mass storage form the logic for the operation of the product, rather than a circuit board of integrated circuits. Data are manipulated through the internal workings of a computer to complete the process rather than a material being reshaped or produced through the internal parts of a machine to manufacture a part.

Possibly, there is truth to the statement that everything changes but also remains the same.

14

Artificial Intelligence in Service

Getting customers involved with the service of their high technology business products can be possible through future applications of artificial intelligence.

Since computers were first introduced, people have envisioned them performing tasks normally requiring human intelligence. This is the area of computer technology commonly referred to as Artificial Intelligence (AI). Recent developments in computer technology now allow computers to store and process much larger amounts of information at much higher rates than ever before. The recent widespread notoriety of artificial intelligence can be attributed to these advances as well as to a general push for the development of practical applications. When leafing through many of the popular technical journals, it is nearly impossible to escape the deluge of articles and advertisements concerned with artificial intelligence products and techniques designed to keep your efforts at the leading edge of technology. But what exactly is artificial intelligence? AI encompasses a variety of state-of-the-art technologies, including expert systems, machine learning, machine vision, voice recognition, and natural language processing. Following a brief description of each area, one can begin to appreciate the benefits of an AI system. Although each AI technology can stand on its own within more conventional technologies, a system incorporating a variety of AI applications stands to reap the greatest benefits.

Expert Systems

At the moment, expert systems have taken the lead in AI research and development efforts due to their potentially high rate of return. Quite simply, an expert system is a computer program that attempts to apply the knowledge and methodology of an expert to solve problems. The implementation of such a system would make expert knowledge readily available for use by anyone at any time. This knowledge could be used to assist users, both experienced personnel and novices, in finding solutions to complex problems. A large number of expert systems have already been developed and are currently in use by industry. The problems attacked by expert systems are quite varied in nature.

Systems exist that are able to customize large computer system configurations to meet individual customer needs. Other systems can perform cable analysis or provide advice for machine lubrication. These successful expert systems have two common factors. First, the problems they solve have numerous variables to consider, and have many solutions, some of which are better than others. Second, the solutions derived by the system are either as good as, or better than a human solution, due to the numerous variables. In most cases, the degree of "goodness" is not the only concern. Consistency of solutions provided by expert systems is also desired. The expert systems of today provide the greatest benefit in areas where expert knowledge is well defined and a large group of people require access to this knowledge.

Natural Language

Natural language processing is an AI technology involved with information exchange. Interacting with a computer traditionally requires the user to enter syntactically constrained information which is understood by the computer. Research is underway that would allow a user to communicate with the computer using normal language-based inquiries. A user attempts to access computer information by posing questions phrased in everyday English, for example. By placing the computer rather than the user in the role of translator, humans would be able to interact with the computer much more quickly and easily.

Voice Recognition

Voice recognition is an area of AI that can promote increased flexibility in the area of machine information exchange. Using this technology, a computer can distinguish words spoken by a user. Although speech synthesis, which is the ability of a computer to speak in a human-like voice, is not an area of AI, we may combine this technology with voice recognition to define the area of voice Input/Output (voice I/O). There are a number of products already on the market that can be used to create voice I/O applications. Products available include voice recognition and synthesis integrated systems. Taking voice I/O one step further, consider combining natural language processing techniques with voice recognition. Undoubtedly, an I/O system reaching the highest degree of flexibility and sophistication would be possible. A computer could distinguish the words spoken by a user as well as understand the information received. Voice I/O could be a very powerful tool in many applications.

Machine Vision

The ability of a computer to recognize visual images in an area of artificial intelligence is commonly referred to as machine vision. The main thrust of this area is to be able to recognize similar objects despite subtle differences in appearance. For example, consider an everyday chair. Every home contains a number of chairs. Each chair has the same function, and most have the basic components which include a seat, a back, and legs. In contrast, each chair can vary from others in size, shape, and even components. Some chairs have arms, others do not. Some chairs have four legs, while others have a single leg with a wide base. The point should be obvious. With today's technology, an object cannot be recognized without an explicit description. A machine vision system would be able to visually *see* an object and, with some information such as basic components and their functionality, it would be able to categorize that object. The development of this area could automate many visually oriented applications.

Machine Learning

Perhaps the most elusive area of AI is machine learning. The ability to make a computer that can reason and make decisions on its own would lead to enormous possibilities. The goal of machine learning is to produce a computer system capable of improving its performance through practice and independent knowledge generation. This could prove useful in both expert systems and other applications. In an expert system, machine learning would enable the system to update its knowledge base continuously by remembering past problems encountered to create new rules and facts, thus more fully emulating a true expert. Using machine learning in conjunction with machine vision would enable a more diverse set of objects to be recognized while decreasing the amount of training necessary for the vision system.

Where Can AI Be Used?

After reviewing the many facets of AI, the basic types of problems that can be solved using this technology begin to emerge. Natural language processing and voice recognition could greatly enhance current information exchange techniques. Expert systems, machine learning, and machine vision could be used to create intelligent systems or systems which solve problems only humans now attack.

Consider an AI-based system for centralized information support. Instead of requiring remotely located personnel to call a centralized station for assistance, such personnel simply converse verbally with a personal portable computer. This portable powerhouse contains not only knowledge, but also an expert system able to evaluate user information to give reasonable advice. If one of the system functions is to solve problems, it will be used to suggest a corrective action after equipment failure has occurred. If the desired results have not been achieved, the system will revise its thought process and continue its investigation until a valid solution is found. In addition, once the correct solution is found, the computer will store this learning experience in memory for future reference.

Applications requiring 24-hour service could be automated so that people are not needed in the hours beyond those of a normal workday. Information exchange would be accomplished using a simulated human voice. Information received from the caller could be processed using voice recognition and natural language processing techniques. The resulting action would depend upon the type of application. This scheme could be used for information retrieval and deposition, or as an intelligent paging system.

Vision systems could be useful in many applications requiring the use of sight. Some obvious application areas include quality control and manufacturing. These systems might also be used to detect changes in objects within a piece of equipment. For instance, consider a small vision system installed within a product that would monitor the wear on mechanical parts. The information derived could be used to determine timely replacement of parts and even recognize design flaws that might be causing unusual wear. On-board vision systems might also be used as an aid for the diagnosis of machine problems. The system could determine the reasons for equipment malfunction by a visual examination of components, recognizing acceptable differences versus irregularities.

Similar Applications

Can an Intelligent System Be Built Today?

In order to answer whether or not an intelligent system can be built today, we must first examine the current state of the AI technologies. The areas which can be said to exist in some tangible form are expert systems, voice recognition, and natural language processing. Machine vision and learning are still not developed to a point where their progress can be accurately measured. With this in mind, let us begin our investigation with a closer look at expert systems.

There are a number of expert system packages, products, and services available on the market today. We can even list quite a few commercially viable systems that are in use. If we take a closer look at these systems, the problems they solve all have a common factor; each problem has a number of correct solutions, some of which are better than others, and each has a well-defined knowledge set. With the present state of the technology, it would be futile to create a system for a problem that lies outside of this domain. The resulting systems would be too unwieldy and unreliable to be feasible. Therefore, it can be said that today the feasibility of an expert system relies on a constraint of application selection.

A similar constraint can be found when reviewing the state of voice recognition. As stated earlier, there are a variety of integrated circuits, printed circuit boards, and systems available for the development of voice recognition applications. Most systems today do a fair job of recognition on the level of speaker dependency. The number of words recognized and rate of recognition depend highly on the product itself. Most of these systems also have the ability to handle some degree of continuous speech. Some newer systems have the ability to manage speaker independence to a certain degree. In essence, voice recognition is progressing at a steady rate. In its current state, the technology can produce limited yet tangible results.

In the realm of AI technologies that can be shown to have made visible progress, natural language processing is the latest to be included. Although the results of investigations in this area have not yet reached the market, there is evidence that they soon will. A glimpse of the product offerings shows that, like voice recognition, limited capability will be the rule. Steady progress should characterize the development of natural language processing, again in much the same way as voice recognition.

Little advance has been made in the areas of machine vision and learning in terms of commercial application. Much research is in progress, with varying results.

It would not be surprising, if after our honest scrutinization of the AI field, one would tend to get pessimistic about the state of AI and the ability to implement an intelligent system. But before making any hasty conclusions, consider again the benefits shown by existing applications. The designers of these systems used originality and imagination to circumvent the inadequacies of present AI technologies to develop seemingly intelligent systems. By realizing the limitations of the tools artificial intelligence has already provided, planning for the development of some useful, but limited, intelligent systems can begin immediately.

Why Pursue the Use of AI?

Although current applications of artificial intelligence technology may be somewhat limited, the technology does present potential for significant cost savings and quality improvements in the near future. Every new technology has had its beginnings entrenched in doubts and disappointments. But this does not mean that the ideas are impossible to achieve. Time is needed for the technology to develop and grow into something of value and usefulness.

The possible applications previously described support and enhance the themes of reliability, flexibility, consistency, and quality already found in these areas. By applying AI techniques to these applications, the resulting systems can provide greater support without increasing personnel requirements. In addition to the cost-effectiveness of these systems, consider the increased marketability gained by using AI technologies. We are all impressed by the expert systems success stories of today. Anyone can produce his or her own success story with a little effort, imagination, and commitment. The key to utilizing artificial intelligence successfully is to remain aware of advances, to use what becomes available along the way, and to convert conventional methods to AI technologies whenever possible.

15

What Is the State of the Art?

State of the art is not all that futuristic. In fact, it is usually available at the local electronics store.

The term *state of the art* is often used to describe new techniques and recent introductions of technology. There are many definitions of what this phrase really means. Webster's dictionary defines state of the art as "the level of development (as of a device, procedure, process, technique, or science) reached at any particular time usually as a result of modern methods." The state of the art in field service technology, then, is the level of development of field service devices, procedures, and techniques. For the purposes of this chapter, however, the term *state of the art* will address those devices, procedures, and techniques that are currently in use and general practice. Methods beyond those currently in use will be considered either experimental or futuristic.

State of the Art

Several service techniques considered to be in the category of state of the art include telemaintenance, where service is accomplished using telephone or data links; the use of portable (transportable), intelligent maintenance devices to deliver service information and diagnostics; constant microcomputer monitoring of equipment performance for instant fault isolation and fault tolerance; and servicing methods such as customer-assisted service.

Futuristic

Cellular telephones, artificial intelligence, and the application of electronic video publications will soon become state of the art, but they still need refinement and improvements in their cost-effectiveness and applications to day-to-day situations before they can be considered as state of the art.

It is interesting, however, to develop future applications for these technologies. As the ability to diagnose equipment failures remotely was an unbelievable and futuristic approach several years ago, the service environment that can be imagined for the future holds equal promise using a combination of these new technologies.

As the products become more complex and sophisticated, they are also becoming simplified. At first, this may seem to be a contradiction. How can products become more complex and yet be simplified? The products are starting to include the capabilities needed by the customer and service people to evaluate the equipment performance, and to understand how it operates internally. Products can do this now to some degree, and they will be better able in the future to correct internal malfunctions and provide their own system backup and redundancy.

The Cost of State-of-the-Art Service

As the cost-per-feature of microelectronic devices continues to decrease, more features and functions not needed for basic product operation, but dedicated to service, are becoming cost-effective. The state of the art in service technology can now become very confusing. Why implement telemaintenance or some portable diagnostic device when the cost of including on-board diagnostics is becoming reasonable? There is no single answer to this question. Each product, marketplace, and organization may find equally attractive solutions while following entirely different approaches to establishing such service philosophies.

Today

Currently, the state of the art in field service technology involves many sophisticated telemaintenance links and a variety of complex tests and diagnostic equipment. The question is, "Are these devices and approaches really state of the art?"

Actually, telemaintenance and other diagnostic delivery devices are just that — delivery devices. In themselves, they add diagnostic elegance, but their greatest impact on product diagnosability is the improvement in on-board diagnostics that they force into the equipment design. Therefore, the state of the art in field service today is driven as much by the service delivery devices as it is by applying computer technology to solving service-related problems.

When the most cost-effective service technique is developed, the service call itself will be either unnecessary or simplified to the point where lesser skilled and lesser trained service personnel will be able to satisfy the customer's servicing needs. In some cases, the customer may even provide his or her own diagnosis and repair. The loss of product availability will be minimized and the probability of first call success in correcting a malfunction will approach 100 percent.

Product Self-Diagnosis

In order to accomplish maximum product availability and first call success, the power of the microcomputer and associated microelectronic components needs to be applied to the diagnosis and service of products. The result will be a product that monitors itself and isolates failures for both the customer and field engineer. Several years ago, the cost of this on-board diagnostic intelligence would have been prohibitive, but today, and even more in the future, this service approach will be a cost-effective approach.

Incorporating the ability for a product to diagnose itself requires careful planning and coordination between design and serviceability engineers. Taking this one step further, many considerations are required to enable the customer to be involved in the service of equipment.

What's Needed?

The necessity for state-of-the-art serviceability features cannot be overstated. To keep the personnel skill level and training requirements to a minimum, all aspects of accessibility, maintainability, and serviceability become increasingly important. Servicing tasks must now be completed by people with less expertise and experience than formerly required. Service people must be able to locate parts, assemblies, and components easily, and also be able to replace these with relative ease. Complex adjustment or alignment procedures reduce customer involvement in service, so they too must be eliminated, or at the very least, minimized.

The technology required to accomplish this state-of-the-art approach to product servicing is available now at a cost-effective level. Successful implementation requires only that there be design goals and that serviceability considerations be taken into account early in the design phase. Although some perceive this as futuristic and beyond the state of the art, it is not. There is no technological reason why the complex components and assemblies in the products designed for the 1980s and 1990s cannot be diagnosed or tested for performance through devices built into the product. This level of product performance evaluation can approach the ultimate service goal, which is, of course, the elimination of the service call entirely.

Summary

The state of the art in product diagnosis and service is the simplification of the service procedure for the field engineer or customer, and the reduction of the number of service tools required to carry out diagnosis and service to a minimum. This requires that each product be capable of monitoring itself, and of determining when and where failures occur. Although this may seem idealistic, the technology is here. It is waiting only for the proper application.

16

The Economics of it All

Service must be cost-effective for the company as well as the customer.

The economics of service have a direct impact on increased earnings, an improved profit margin, and an increased return on investment (or a more profitable product line). The role that service plays in the overall economics of a product is often overlooked and many times not properly estimated. This chapter addresses the influence service has in determining the profitability of a product, and indicates some areas where the cost of service needs to be carefully assessed.

Extra, and Maybe an Unnecessary, Cost?

The design required to provide better service is often considered to be an extra, and sometimes unnecessary, cost. This is especially true during the product design stage. Adding sensors (to circuits and mechanical components), performance indicators, or feedback circuitry all contribute to the final cost of manufacturing a product. Design and manufacturing engineers try to develop low-cost products, and service features seem to be hindering these efforts.

The service features must be proven cost-effective in order to be incorporated into the product. An important consideration is the one-time design cost associated with these features, compared to the ongoing product life cycle returns in reduced-service demand.

Life Cycle Costs

In evaluating the economics of a service procedure or of a service technique, the costs and savings over the entire product life cycle must be considered. Several items contributing to the cost of service are:

- The additional circuitry required in the product to support the testing and diagnosis of equipment failures.
- The diagnostic software required to exercise the components making up the product.
- The test and repair equipment required to evaluate circuit, component, and overall product performance.
- The service publications.
- The service training.
- The required parts inventory.
- The additional operating and overhead items such as transportation costs, telephone costs, etc.

In addressing techniques that can be used to reduce service costs and overhead, or in justifying specific service technologies or procedures, reductions in the cost of the items listed previously (that comprise the cost of service) need to be identified. These will be considered in three categories: reducing call frequency, reducing call duration, and reducing parts demand. The actual economic considerations for each item will overlap, since there are common elements in each area. However, in general terms, their relationship and economics will be more directly influenced by the specific product than by the service approach.

Call Frequency

Increased call frequency naturally results in substantially higher service costs. The call frequency is often thought to be a function of equipment reliability. This is true to a certain extent, but at the same time, actual call frequency is influenced greatly by many of the items that contribute to the cost of service. Call frequency is also determined by how well prepared the service person is to complete the repair properly on the first call. A repeat call can occur days or even weeks after the original call and be a direct result of the quality of the service performed on the original call. The quality of training, service procedures, diagnostic procedures, parts, and the thoroughness of product-performance testing all influence call frequency.

Ideally, every problem would be correctly diagnosed and properly repaired during the first call, but this is not always the case. Even more serious is the number of problems caused by a poorly trained and equipped field engineer in completing the call. A person not completely trained and familiar with the system (or user) aspects of a product can inadvertently induce equipment malfunctions while attempting to remedy a problem. These repeat calls are often confused with poor or unsatisfactory equipment reliability. No design changes will improve this situation unless they are aimed at testability and serviceability. Improving this situation requires a systems approach to problem isolation and correction, where all aspects of operation and interaction are thoroughly understood.

Call Duration

When call duration is considered, the service design objective is often simply to reduce the duration of the service call to a minimum. The important point to remember in attempting to reduce call duration is that there is a minimum that cannot be eliminated. Several elements that contribute to this minimum include: travel time to the customer location, customer relations time (the time it takes the customer to explain the problem and the time required to explain the repair to the customer), and the time to evaluate proper equipment performance before leaving the equipment site. This minimum call duration does not include the diagnostic and repair time because there would be none involved during the minimum duration service call. Testability, diagnosability, serviceability, and effective parts-stocking measures only influence the duration of service calls involving diagnosis and repair.

The Minimum Service Call

When considering the diagnostic and repair time savings attributed to testability, diagnostic, and serviceability techniques, the savings can never eliminate the minimum service call. This minimum can only be influenced through complete elimination of the service call (the first call or the repeat call).

Improved training of service personnel and customers, and improved equipment performance evaluation after a repair, will help to eliminate these "unnecessary" service calls.

Parts

Replacement parts (those carried by the field engineer whether they are needed or not) can play a major role in the final cost of providing effective service. Parts commonality and the ability to interchange electronic printed circuit boards reduce the economic burden on service costs caused by the parts. In order to be effective and to minimize these expenses, not only is careful planning necessary, but a knowledge of the existing products in the marketplace by the service engineer is required for developing recommendations for replacement parts.

As mentioned earlier, supplying parts to the field engineer creates what is called the parts pipeline. This pipeline can dramatically increase the overall costs of supplying support for a product. It becomes an even more costly element when OEM (Original Equipment Manufacturers) parts are elements in the pipeline. The pipeline, sometimes referred to as "board float" for printed circuit boards, can contribute greatly to the total parts inventory. An inefficient pipeline can drive the inventory values to substantial dollar amounts, where a significant percentage of a company's assets can be committed to the parts pipeline. The most economical solution to the cost of the pipeline will vary, depending on the characteristics of the actual pipeline. The methods that address problems in a pipeline having a large volume of the same type of boards may not be effective for replacement parts pipelines having a large volume of different board types. Steps to reduce the parts in the pipeline should not be ignored when attempting to minimize overall service costs.

Trade-Offs

The economics of service and product support become very complex when all issues are considered. Overlooking one of these issues during service design can have a significant impact on overall service costs. While inventories need to be kept to a minimum, an adequate supply of replacement parts is required to minimize repeat (or return) service calls and to provide maximum product availability (up time). Trade-offs need to be made between the duration of the service call and the level of service performed. The exchange of major assemblies may reduce the time required to diagnose and repair a malfunction, but the cost of these major assemblies may prohibit this servicing approach, or at least make it less attractive.

These are only some of the challenges faced by the serviceability engineers who are attempting to develop realistic and cost-effective service procedures and approaches. Additional considerations are encountered when sophisticated test equipment is required to evaluate the performance of a product.

The Computer...Again

Before beginning the actual cost analysis, a series of decisions regarding the profile of the intended service support are needed. Defined service goals are an absolute necessity. This requires good service planning. The plan should include the desired call frequency, call duration, response time, replacement part and distribution objectives, the skills required by the field engineer to perform equipment evaluation and repair, and assumptions regarding the training and publications support levels necessary. This will help in establishing a base from which to work in determining the economic impact of the additional test equipment and service procedures. The analysis now becomes a series of economic trade-offs, since, in the most basic repair situation product substitution or product replacement could be adapted to effect repair. However drastic a service measure this may seem, replacing a product may be the most cost-effective service solution.

Elements of a Cost Analysis

The actual cost analysis should address the following items:

- Present after-tax values and the after-tax cash flow rate of return expected from the implemented service technique.
- Development and application expenses for the technique, tool, or service procedure as they relate to the product.
- Capital acquisition costs and depreciation considerations for the test equipment and support equipment.
- Exchange parts and regular parts inventory costs, both expended and saved.
- The repair costs of the product with and without the new test equipment.
- Training costs for service personnel both with and without the service technique or tool.
- The salaries of service personnel required to support the product with or without the service techniques or tools.
- Software maintenance expenses for diagnostic software resident in the product and diagnostic software external to the product.

- Revenue lost from reduced sales of parts and from the reduction in the need for service by customers with products out of warranty.
- Savings realized from reduced installation and equipment setup times.
- Inventory (replacement parts) and pipeline costs and possible reductions in both of these areas.
- Savings in periodic maintenance times for equipment in warranty and for equipment covered by service contracts.
- The diminished need to purchase alternative test equipment or increase the volume of existing equipment currently being used.
- Revenue from the sale of test equipment to customers who perform their own service and maintenance.
- The influence on the service person's learning curve.
- The duplication and distribution of software for the test equipment or the service technique.
- The application of the test equipment or the service technique to support other current and future products.
- The estimated useful life of the test equipment and the life of the product being supported.
- The anticipated effect of the test equipment on call duration, call frequency, travel time, and return or repeat calls.

Summary

Developing a cost analysis around the elements mentioned previously will provide a starting point for an evaluation of the financial impact of implementing new service techniques or test equipment to improve product support and service. The results will be a key element in setting the direction for supporting sophisticated products in the future. However, the service engineer must remain sensitive to several considerations beyond strictly economic issues that must be reviewed to achieve the desired efficiency in product service and support.

17

Project Planning—The Key to Meeting Your Objectives

Plan, plan, plan...everyone needs a plan.

The phrase, "If you don't know where you are going, any path will get you there," really says it all when the subject of project planning is reviewed. To know where you are going, all efforts need to be directed on specific paths toward meeting the objectives. The element that provides this direction is the project plan.

The planning process should result in a clear path to follow to obtain objectives. Generally, the value of the plan is directly related to the stability of the project and the organization. The less stable or more complex the project or the organization, the more a solid plan is needed. Plans are essential when competitive and technical environments are in strategic flux. Strategic flux, unfortunately, is the case in many aspects of business.

Planning for a project is a nonlinear activity, where all the phases of a plan are occurring simultaneously. Plans usually don't have a distinct beginning, middle, and end, although many people believe that their plan does have three distinct elements.

A close review of all plans will show how the beginning, middle, and end are not as distinct as generally thought when the influence of project plan contingencies is considered. Every contingency has the potential to cause modification of the project plan. Selecting and implementing contingencies will change the beginning, middle, and end of the project plan.

Although all projects are subject to events that can be considered and usually are, in fact, catastrophic to the objectives of the project, effective planning can keep a large percentage of these events from occurring. The critical element is making good contingency plans.

Contingency plans are often overlooked, since many plans call for an "all success" program. "What if" exercises are truly valuable in assessing the impact of various events on any given project. If these events can be foreseen, and a plan developed for them, their impact will be kept to a minimum.

Project plans have value to others beyond the immediate personnel involved in the project. The plan provides the following to a project and an organization:

- A path or course of action to follow.
- Proof to corporate management of the soundness of our judgment.
- Help in identifying critical issues and developing contingencies.
- Improvement in operational effectiveness by creating standards to measure progress.
- Reduction of the likelihood of failure due to management error.

Good project plans have distinctive characteristics. If the plan lacks several of the essential characteristics, the value of the plan will be in question. Without a solid plan, there will be some areas of the organization or some individuals involved in the project who will not be made aware of their roles and responsibilities.

A list of planning characteristics is provided as a thought-provoker for the planner. This list is intended to be general, and therefore, addresses requirements that will vary from organization to organization. The actual characteristics that will satisfy good planning processes need to be developed for each specific organizational area.

Planning Characteristics

- Planning phases are interdependent and each phase affects every other phase.
- Planning is an interactive process, since the planner must start where he or she is and test each idea or concept against the goals of the plan.
- A plan is valid only at the moment of conception and is, therefore, dynamic.
- Plans are unique and represent the documentation proving a specific planner's case for a specific action.
- Organizational objectives drive the entire system. Business can only reduce its organizational objectives to a single, simple,

and overwhelming objective when it is in the survival mode. With many objectives, there is a good chance of conflicting objectives, for example, increase service offerings while reducing costs. These conflicting objectives establish the trade-off dimensions for operational management, based on the initial objectives coming from top management.

- A situation analysis will establish where we are.
- The clients must be identified along with the areas of concentration.
- Plans should identify strengths and weaknesses.
- Plans should emphasize strategy and tactics.

Two activities that take a large amount of time during the planning process are the strategy development and the tactic development activities. A plan will be only as good as the supporting strategies and tactics.

Major plan objectives are (and should be) impossible to change without altering the entire process. In other words, if the primary objective changes so will the entire plan to reach that objective.

It is essential that firm goals be set. Once the goals are set, the plan is used dynamically to attain the goals. The dynamics come into play when a particular course of action proves to be unreasonable. Knowing the relationship between all of the intermediate goals is essential in modifying the plan to correct the errant course of action.

Strategies are planning steps at a level below that of planning objectives. Strategies can be modified only with a dramatic change in other parts of the plan. Strategies are developed with specific objectives in mind, and are supported by the tactics of the plan. Strategy development flows from the following items:

- Recognizing important strategic opportunities and threats identified by a situation analysis.

- Combining the probability of occurrence with the potential impact of the event to measure each opportunity and threat.

- Prioritizing the list of opportunities to form an implicit statement of strategy or, more simply, what we want to do.

The basic element in a project plan is the tactic. Tactics can be changed much more easily than strategies, and will not have as devastating an influence on the project as will changing strategies. The contingencies developed generally support changes in tactics. If better methods are developed to address the needs of the strategies, the tactics may be modified. The tactics may be developed while carrying out the following:

- Answering the question of what it is we are going to do to make the strategy happen.
- Identifying the resources it will take and the price it will cost.
- Describing how the results will be promoted.
- Determining how we will budget and control to maximize the chances of success.

To prepare a thorough, comprehensive plan for any project, several elements should be considered for the plan. Not all elements or components are generally needed for all planning efforts and for each plan, but larger project plans or project proposals require attention to most, if not all, of the following listed components. Actually, proposing and managing a project is very much like proposing and managing a small business. The elements are:

1. The Management Summary
   - Must be positive and persuasive.
   - Is a "sales pitch" for what we want to do.
   - Is generally written last.

2. Organization and Projects
   - Gives an overview of the organization.
   - Tells how we fit.
   - Tells what we do.
   - Lists past successes.

3. Service Industry Analysis
   - Tells what is out there.
   - Tells why we are taking a particular direction in service.
   - Explains how we can do better than "the rest."

4. Environmental Analysis
   - Explains the risk of being nontraditional.
   - Lists the benefits of success.

5. The Plan
   - Gives the philosophy of how we can do it.
   - Lists the stages of the plan.
   - Outlines the milestones.

6. Development Plans
   - List longer term opportunities and tell how to get them.
   - List contingencies.

7. Operational Plans
   - Give proof of how we can manage day-to-day events to achieve plan objectives.
   - Give proof we can deliver the results.

8. The Management Team
   - Tells who's who.
   - Tells who's needed
   - Lists the skills required.
   - Reviews the positions and skills.

9. Overall Schedule
   - Is reasonably estimated on a period-by-period basis.
   - Contains details of each phase.
   - Has critical decision milestones.

10. Critical Risks and Problems
    - Evaluate on the basis of potential impact.
    - Discuss contingencies for each risk.

11. The Financial Plan
    - Includes NPV (Net Present Value).
    - Gives CFRR (Cash Flow Rate of Return).
    - Gives cost versus savings.

12. The Offering
    - Is a one-page summary of needs versus results.
    - Tells what the product really is and what it really means to the service industry and the company.

Probably one of the best ways to understand how strategies and tactics can be developed to support a plan is to review an actual project plan. The following project "To Dig a Hole" is an example that brings out the application of several of the planning processes discussed. Although the project itself is simple in its objective, the discussion of the elements in the plan serves to further define the basics of project planning. Even though the source of the quotation is long forgotten, it was once stated that "planning is really common sense in action." This is still true today.

Planning For a Project, or How to Dig a Hole

The Project

There is a need to dig a hole in the front of the building where we all work. It is a very large hole and could be a very deep hole. In any case, the project must be planned and executed in the most productive manner possible. The plan should use the minimum number of resources and the project must remain on schedule to be successful.

Setting the Objective

To establish the objective, we first have to decide what we want to accomplish and then express that in clearly understood, measurable terms. In this project, the objective may be to dig a hole.

In itself, the objective, to dig a hole, describes the project to everyone, but in terms that do not adequately define the goals of the project. We need to be more specific in our objective so that we will be able to measure it and know when we meet the objective. With this objective, we won't know when we are done. We won't know if the hole is the correct size and at the correct location. Finally, the objective doesn't even help us determine what resources will be needed (manpower and equipment).

When we establish an objective for a project, the objective must be specific as to what, why, where, and when. The project plan will then add the "how" element to complete our understanding of the project.

A more useful project objective may be as follows: to dig a hole that is X feet deep and Y feet in diameter, located Z inches in front of the main entrance to the building by next Thursday.

Planning the Project

In planning the project, one of the first tasks should be to review the objective and to develop strategies to allow for the attainment of the objective. The strategies must then be supported by several operating tactics. These become the "how to" steps to implementation.

Through this planning, the project needs can be identified. Since there is a reasonable understanding of the objective of this project, the strategies can now be developed.

Project Strategies

The following are examples of the strategies that could be used to obtain the project objective. There will be other strategies that come to mind, but they should only be considered if the project objective changes significantly.

Strategy 1. Survey location of the hole and mark with appropriate stakes.

Strategy 2. Use manpower to excavate earth, using manual tools including picks, shovels, and prybars.

Strategy 3. Remove dirt from site, using wheelbarrows.

Project Tactics

The strategies must be supported by tactics, which are the detailed "how to" steps leading to the completion of the project. The tactics are more flexible than the strategies and can be modified without a major impact on the completion of the project.

Tactic 1. Contract with ABC Survey Company for the survey of the hole. This must be completed by Tuesday at noon to be sure to meet the project schedule.

Tactic 2. Hire 10 workers to excavate dirt, based on calculations of an eight-hour day, two and a half working days, and known worker productivity.

Tactic 3. Rent five wheelbarrows of one cubic yard capacity each, for removal of excavated dirt in order to remove the dirt in two and a half working days.

Tactic 4. Rent five shovels and picks, and purchase three prybars for completing the excavation.

Tactic 5. Appoint one worker as foreman to oversee the project.

Project Contingencies

In spite of the fact that we have planned carefully for this project, there are several outside influences that can affect the completion of the project on time and within the projected cost. Some of these influences can be predicted or forecast as possibilities, while other events may occur which we can't predict or maybe even imagine. In order to deal with these problems, we must develop contingency plans.

Contingency 1. If we are delayed by rainy weather, then...

Contingency 2. If large, immovable rocks are found during the excavation, then...

Contingency 3. If the required labor can't be hired, then...

(A contingency should be developed for each element of the plan that could influence our success in completing the project.)

Carrying Out the Project

With a solid objective, sound strategies, reasonable and practical tactics, and well thought out contingencies, the project has a good chance of being successful. However, even with all of the careful planning that has gone into this activity, there is still a need for strong leadership to implement the plan and to activate contingencies as necessary.

Without a well-designed plan, leadership will not make the project a success, and without strong leadership, the plan will, by itself, not create a successful project. Successful projects have plans that are implemented by people in organizations with documented goals and effective leadership. For an organization to be successful, four organizational terms must be defined. These terms are:

- *Mission.* The specific function of the organization.
- *Objective.* The goal of the course of action.
- *Method.* What are the procedures to obtain the objective?
- *Scope.* The area or range of the group's activities.

When these terms are defined and understood by the members of the organization, the expectations of each individual must be made clear. People must know exactly what is expected of them in all cases. They must also be able to relate these expectations to the organizational terms listed previously in a manner that motivates them to do a good job.

A test of how well individual expectations have been defined is when an immediate answer can be given to the following questions:

- What are you doing?
- Why are you doing it?
- When will you be finished?

It is often very interesting to listen to the "average" employee try to answer these three simple questions. Often their responses will be either very general or very detailed. In each case, the essence of their responsibilities is seldom addressed. The following is an example of the average response given to these questions, and the preferred way of viewing an individual's contributions.

- What are you doing?

  Average response: Writing a diagnostic program.

  Preferred response: Contributing to the diagnostic capabilities for XYZ product.

- Why are you doing it?

  Average response: Because it is in the specifications.

  Preferred response: To reduce the time to isolate a failure in the ABC subassembly.

- When will you be finished?

  Average response: Later this week.

  Preferred reaponse: In time to provide the routine as a part of the QC test package which is due later this week.

The way people review their responsibilities and the resulting ways they meet expectations are critical to all organizations' success. Often, the only change necessary to motivate people to do a better job is to change their view or their expectations. People at all levels must understand the value of their individual contributions to the overall success of a project and their department.

Summary

What is needed to be truly successful is, first, an objective that is specific enough for all to understand. Second, there should be a plan of how to reach the objective that is visible to everyone. Finally, we need the manpower and leadership to "make it happen."

18

The Future

The future of service in an organization may well be the future of the organization itself.

Preparing for the future is at best the development of a series of predictions, forecasts, strategies, and tactics. There are far too many uncontrollable contributing factors to permit precise estimates and solid forecasts. However, preparations can be made to better position ourselves to deal with the future, and the only thing we know for certain is that *there will be change*. This change will, of course, be technological, but should also include the way the service business is organized and managed. Holding on to current and past philosophies and procedures can only encourage inflexibility and eventual failure. As all aspects of our environment change, the service environment will also change. Several approaches that will allow for adaptation to this change are presented here for their thought-provoking value. Some may apply, while others may not, but they are alternatives.

Purchase Decisions

Service is, and will continue to be, a significant factor in any major purchase decision. Companies with the more aggressive sales strategies will increasingly emphasize service support as a major portion of a product offering. This is becoming true for both professional business and consumer products. If companies desire more sales and a larger market share, they will have to provide new levels of service for their products to achieve this goal. Customers are expecting increasingly large percentages of up time (availability) from products they purchase. The only way to provide this, beyond initial product reliability, is through an excellent service support plan and service offering. Diagnostic and repair times, first call repair efficiency, and short response times are becoming critical in the determination and perception of the quality of the service provided. In order to provide customers with improved service in the future, there are several changes that can be made in the approach to service. Some of these possibilities are outlined in the following sections.

Customer Support Centers

The service assistance support center has become a way of providing service in the computer industry. A customer calls the center for assistance and is directed through a series of tests (that the customer can perform) to help isolate a problem. This is sometimes referred to as customer-assisted service. The important point is that the customer becomes involved in the maintenance of his or her product. Home appliance manufacturers first began providing this support to allow the customer to remedy the less complex problems and increase the up time of their products. While benefitting the customer, this assistance also eliminates costly service calls, especially during the warranty period, and gives the customer "ownership" of the product.

Carry-In Service Centers

Another innovative approach involves carry-in, or messenger service. Service centers for carry-in service allow for an efficient service operation and a minimal service time. The technical staff of the carry-in service center can be more effectively used through a constant flow of product. The burden of travel, in the true carry-in operation, is placed on the customer.

Messenger service places the burden of travel on the servicing unit, but frees the skilled service personnel to concentrate on product diagnosis and repair, since messengers deliver the product from the customer to these service locations and, after the repair is completed, back to the customer. The messengers are typically not skilled service personnel, but are trained only to assist the customer with operational problems.

Self-Diagnosis

The future holds promise for not only how service is accomplished, but also for the role of a product in its own diagnosis. Several manufacturers are currently promoting the capability of their products to isolate malfunctions and report them to the users. This is often based on the concepts of artificial intelligence or the nonhuman decision process. Future products will incorporate more and more features (both service-related and non-service-related), based on the concept of artificial intelligence, which will allow products to test and diagnose themselves.

Artificial Intelligence

Exactly what constitutes an artificial intelligence system is not well-defined. In the basic sense, any decision made by electronic or nonhuman means represents an application of artificial intelligence. Although this definition may seem too broad, when one considers the confusion in defining a knowledge-based system, or an expert system, along with artificial intelligence, the problems of definition become greater. So, for the purpose of the future service environment, it is safe to say only that the products will play an increasingly active role in monitoring their internal performance. Ideally, between the assistance provided by the customer in servicing the product, and the assistance provided by in-product intelligence, the service burden will be lessened for all but the most complex failures.

Service Development

Corporations (primarily the service organizations) need to prepare for the future service technologies. New technologies incorporated into the product design are often the result of research or development efforts. Large amounts of money are expended to make sure that the products are developed to the current state of the art. A similar effort is required to make sure that service is developed to the current state of the art.

Research and development into service technologies will allow the service organization to effectively address the service challenges presented by technologically advanced products. The service issues cannot become afterthoughts or compromises to the product design. New and unique methods need to be explored which help test and diagnose the complex and advanced equipment technologies. Past and current attempts are often compromised when used in the new environments. Without dedication (at the corporate level) to developing new service approaches, cost-effective and efficient service procedures will not be possible.

Organization

Service management and the service organizational structure itself need to be ready for the future. As the role of service becomes more influential in product sales and company revenues, how the service organization is positioned within a company is increasingly important. A service organization that is aligned with design and manufacturing groups is vulnerable to losing its focus on service issues and begins concentrating on design and manufacturing efficiencies at the expense of service features. Regardless of organizational structure or positioning, the service organization must concentrate its focus on the customer and marketing. Since service is performed at the request of, and for the benefit of the customer, the customer focus is critical to a service organization's survival.

Sales and Service

Service is not only a contributor to revenues and earnings through direct charges for the service performed, but is an ever-increasing contributor to revenues through product sales. A service plan which supports products is often the deciding factor in the customer decision to purchase from one vendor or another. Based on this close link with product sales, the service organization can contribute most effectively. Sales and service need to be closely related. They have been in the past, and will need to continue to be in the future. Advances in service technology may even make it feasible to have the sales and service functions performed by the same person.

A Corporate Identity

The effectiveness of a service organization can be improved through its position in the corporate structure. As just discussed, service is closely linked to product sales, but also requires close contact with design and manufacturing. These interfaces are necesary because service and serviceability influence every stage of a product's life cycle.

Service is a strategic element of a business. Service management should be an integral and independent part of the strategic planning process. Service management also should be an integral partner in the decision-making process of the business units or corporation.

Summary

The future success of servicing new and innovative products depends in part on the service organization's ability to develop or adapt new and innovative service approaches and techniques to future products. Future success also requires that service management, correctly positioned in the corporate structure, meets the challenges presented by the sophisticated products that are emerging. The future demands a combination of salesmanship and service with research, development, and innovation — especially innovation.

It was once stated, when referring to recent advances in computer technology, that, "If we have the brainpower to invent these machines, we have the brainpower to make certain they are a boon and not a bane to humanity."

A futuristic vision of field service is developed in the next chapter. One can readily see that the possibilities are almost endless.

19

A Focus on the Technologies of the Future

Technology may well provide the solution to the dilemma technology created.

Technological change has created many new opportunities for improvements in the ways that service is delivered and in the ways that service is performed. Everyone involved in the service business will be influenced by new technology applications to service problems. As the complexities of products increase, the complexities of the service approaches need to change to keep service offerings competitive. The opportunities for improved product service are limited only by the imagination. Some approaches, however, are closer to being realized and represent developments in the not-too-distant future. Some will be implemented, while others may not, but all have the potential to help the service organization achieve quality, cost-effective service.

Predictive Maintenance

When the required service can be predicted before it is needed, service planning will take on a new meaning. All machines containing mechanical components wear out. Being able to determine the rate of wear and the amount of life remaining in an assembly will allow field service to be planned as never before. This predictive maintenance can be accomplished through the application of several technologies.

The use of acoustic sensors to monitor the frequency of sounds generated by mechanical components that move will help to isolate components that will soon require replacement or repair. The signals generated by these acoustic sensors, which are "listening" for component failures, can be analyzed by portable diagnostic computing devices that will determine the remaining useful life of the component.

The field service person could possibly replace parts that are about to cause failures during the current service call or could bring the about-to-be-needed parts on a future call. In either case, service calls will be avoided and the customer will have improved product availability.

Fault-Tolerant Computers

A majority of the functions performed by complex products are controlled by the software portion of the product. This software operates in the microelectronic sections of the product where literally millions of decisions are made each second. Only through computer applications can an accurate problem diagnosis be made. In some computing systems today, and in more systems in the future, these computers will be able to create alternative operating modes to continue operation once a fault is determined.

In some computer systems, redundant circuitry provides a means of continuing operation after a fault has occurred. In other systems, operation continues, but at reduced efficiency, until repairs can be made. Fault-tolerant systems provide a means for operation when these computer systems fail. They also provide the service organization the ability to plan service better, since the customers will not lose the total functioning of the product.

Product-Initiated Remote Diagnostics

The technology required to make diagnostics available from a central location separate from the customer's equipment is available and in use today. The future applications of this technology will add new meaning to the term remote diagnostics.

One of the goals in good service planning is to reduce the MTTR. At first, this goal may be equated with reducing call duration, and then expanded to include reductions in travel time and eventually response time. Product-initiated remote diagnostics will allow the service organization to take all of this one step further and allow the MTTR to be viewed as the time between the moment of failure and when the product is operating to specification.

All failures occur before the customer realizes there has been a failure. In some cases, this time may be only seconds, while in other cases this may be much longer. Intelligence incorporated in the service features of a product can detect failures often before the failure is evident to the customer. This intelligence could then initiate a call for service to a central computer. The central computer could either dispatch a service person, or perform a series of diagnostic tests to isolate the source of the problem. In either case, the future application of product-initiated remote diagnostics will reduce the MTTR to a point that will provide maximum response to a customer's problem.

A Portable Computer "Tool Box"

As the technological complexity in the products serviced increases, the tools and test equipment required also increases. If this were to continue, the service person would not be able to carry all the test equipment necessary to service a product. Portable computers can be adapted to address this problem and provide the necessary intelligent test equipment for such complex service situations.

Several equipment manufacturers offer intelligent diagnostic instruments for specific functions. In the future, advances in electronic component density will allow these to become smaller and more portable. One could imagine several instruments combined into a single hand-held device that could supply the field service person the capability to perform tests now done by an oscilloscope, voltmeter, logic analyzer, and communications interface testing device in one package.

The most important feature of this portable computer may not be the diagnostic tests that it can perform, but the data it displays. Using artificial intelligence technology, this portable computer will be able to deliver analyzed data to the user. The complexity of the products serviced is making analysis of the data displayed difficult, at best. Analyzed data will greatly improve the diagnostic process for the service person.

Communications Technologies

Of all the technological advances that will affect field service, advances in communications technology may have the most impact. The world is becoming a "real time" environment where information is needed almost instantly at various places. This need for fast, cost-effective communications exists throughout the service business. Field engineers need to contact their office, the customer, or other field engineers for information necessary to their job. The future promise for many service technologies is dependent on communications between products and central diagnostic computers. The local service office needs to be able to contact both field engineers and customers in a timely manner. All of this depends on efficient communications systems. Advances in communications technology will provide these systems.

The use of cellular telephones is becoming common in many areas today. In the not-too-distant future, cellular modems will be a reality. This technology will allow data transmission without depending on telephone cables and land lines. The logical step beyond current technology is to incorporate satellite communications with these cellular modems and, therefore, make point-to-point communications available anywhere in the country. With this technology, a service person could communicate with any other service person or support system by simply using a portable hand-held device. Data and information will truly be available in real time!

The potential benefits and applications of new communications technologies are fast becoming reality. They have the capability of changing the way the service organization conducts business and provides the customers with quality service.

Summary

Changes in field service technology will have an impact on the way that service is provided and on the way that the service organization functions. New technologies do not limit but expand the role of the field engineer in providing cost-effective, quality service. Service will always be required at the customer's site. A concern for and a focus on the needs of the customer will always be key success factors in a quality service organization. The application of technology will only help the service organization in meeting customer expectations.

20

Summing it Up

Proactive service approaches are needed today in all areas of the service organization.

Servicing techniques that deal with advanced technologies will make concepts such as those described a necessity, not a luxury. Automobile manufacturers are designing multiple CPU systems, interconnected by communications networks to control the basic operation of their vehicles. Home entertainment products rely on computer technology to provide sophisticated options and features. The increasing complexity of products and the technologies that make these products possible, combined with the increasing dependence on these technologies, are going to demand more and more from service organizations.

The service organization of the future must be prepared to cope with the products that technology has made possible. An approach to coping with this environment is to incorporate the very same technologies into the support of field service. There must be technology in field service.